CHILE

ALLENDE AND AFTER

George Protopapas

Our Sunday Visitor, Inc.
Huntington, Indiana 46750

ISBN: 0-87973-772-7
Library of Congress Catalog Card Number: 74-29467

Cover Design by James E. McIlrath

Published, printed and bound in the U.S.A. by
Our Sunday Visitor, Inc.
Noll Plaza
Huntington, Indiana 46750

772

Contents

Preface

Although I am a citizen of the United States, I have lived for the last fifteen years in Chile, excepting a few vacations at home. For the last three years, except for a few trips to Brazil and Argentina of three to four weeks' duration, I have been continually residing in Chile.

I was living in Santiago when the military coup of September 11, 1973, took place. In this book I want to relate what I saw with my own eyes, the events that took place as I personally observed them, and my personal experiences during the three years of President Allende's term and during the first year of the new military regime.

Two events prompt me to write. I was asked by a friend attending an international meeting for a report on the situation in Chile. I accepted gladly because the reports of the international press seemed to me to be wholly lacking in objectivity, even to be notoriously false on many occasions. The other event that made me put everything aside for three months — I was busy doing research in economic development — started with a telephone call from a woman asking that I find asylum in an embassy for her husband who was in serious trouble with the Military Junta. The news that I could be of some help traveled quickly. Before I knew it I was besieged by people from as far north as Iquique and as far south as Valdivia, begging me to help them find asylum in an embassy for themselves or for a relative or friend. Others simply came to tell me of their sufferings, their persecution by the military, the tortures they had been subjected to, of the loss of their jobs, and similar stories.

In writing this book I have but one aim: to describe as objectively and impartially as possible why the military coup took place and what has been happening ever since in Chile. What I relate is never from hearsay but always from personal experience and personal investigation. The cases I report are those which were personally presented to me and which I personally verified. In some instances, I have changed names and surnames for obvious reasons and have simplified in a considerable degree cases I present. When I say that the poor have been greatly affected by the new economic measures of the Junta, I base my conclusions not solely on an economic point of view but also on an existential point of view. I have seen firsthand how the poor suffer in body and spirit since the adoption of these new measures.

Probably there are some slight discrepancies in the cases I report. However, they do not affect in any way the truth of what is said. The lapses are inconsequential details of location, or of time, which do not affect the substance of what is related. If there are any substantial errors, they are involuntary ones for which I apologize. As for the interpretation of the events, this is personal and therefore subjective.

The book at first glance may appear to many as purely negative in outlook. In the first part, I criticize Allende, his *Unidad Popular* (U.P.), its social, economic and political policies, the Catholic priests and laity of the left; in the second section of the book, I do the same in regard to the Armed Forces, their government, the priests and Catholics of the right.

The Armed Forces, just as did the U.P. from 1970 to 1973, are trying to force people to conform to a program without taking into consideration the dignity of the human person and the inviolability of conscience. The new leaders forget, as the U.P. did, that no change imposed from the outside is accepted if it is not first interiorized. The Armed Forces are going to lose gradually their credibility as a government, as did the U.P., because of their lack of solidarity with all the Chileans. If the Armed Forces do not alter their course of action, they will find, as the U.P. did too late, that the support of the masses is indispensable precisely at the moment when it begins to fail them.

The errors that the U.P. committed and the evil supposedly it was preparing to do, the Armed Forces are perpetuating in part today. It is a vicious circle that leads nowhere except to disaster.

I sent the first draft of this manuscript (the last chapters contained only the germinal ideas of what I developed at length in this book) to the President of the Junta, General Augusto Pinochet, whom I had known when he was commander of a regiment in Antofagasta; his children attended the college where I was rector at the time.

I was told to go ahead and publish it, but with the corrections made by the Secretary of the Press. The last chapters had been removed from the manuscript. Under those conditions, I decided not to publish it in Chile. The book would have given a deformed view of the Chilean reality. The book would have been as unbalanced and as biased in favor of the military as the reports of the international press in favor of Allende. I would print all or nothing. I have opted to print all — outside of Chile.

As I have said, I try to be as impartial a witness as possible of the events prior to the military coup of September 11, 1973, and the events since.

It is my contribution, I hope, to the reconstruction of Chile.

George Protopapas
Santiago, Chile

Introduction

"When at the end of 1972 the then President of Chile, Salvador Allende, traveled to more than three continents and spoke before the United Nations in New York, the general impression he gave of his government and his mission was excellent.

"The Chilean Socialist experience was looked upon as unique in the world and as an example to follow by other Latin-American countries. Everyone from the exterior looked at the 'process' with great interest and predicted for it a very successful future.

"Those of us who accompanied Allende on that memorable trip were stunned to see that Allende enjoyed such a high reputation in the world at large, and that his government was considered as an example to follow. At home his popularity had fallen; discontent was rampant and the specter of a civil war loomed ever more clearly on the horizon. . . .

"Allende spoke of a 'democratic and pluralistic Socialism.' In his speeches he showed himself respectful of bourgeois institutionality and the democratic political system. At times he dramatically pleaded to put aside the differences that could plunge the country into a civil war.

"The image that the world had of Allende was one of a progressive President doing his utmost to raise the level of the poor, of a courageous statesman who had the audacity to do battle with the huge multinational companies and claim for his people the right to economic independence. He was looked upon as a liberator, as the most representative leader of the Third World.

"People in Mexico, Colombia, France, Spain, the United States and Africa spoke sympathetically about Allende. Even those opposed to Communism and Socialism joined in and . . . supported him. . . .

"Thus it is that Allende's fall from power was received with consternation and frustration. It could only be explained in terms of plots, conjurations, by external enemy forces, such as the CIA, or the multinational corporations, such as the ITT.

"The truth of the matter is that the Chilean Socialist experiment was a 'flop.' It expired not because of external pressures, but because the people of Chile themselves put an end to it.

"The Chileans had tremendous confidence in Allende at the beginning of his term. They believed in him; they believed in his program; they believed that he would put an end to injustice. His electoral support rose from 36% in the presidential election to 50% in the municipal election of April, 1971, six months after winning the Presidential elections.

"The stark truth is, however, that in spite of the many opportunities he had, he failed to fulfill his promises. On the contrary, he let his political assessors lead him astray. . . .

"Allende maintained the democratic system, but he violated the spirit of democracy. What Allende said and preached abroad was one thing; what he did in Chile was another. Allende failed because he operated on two levels: a level of law and formality, and a level of intrigues and Machiavellic practices."

Emilio Filippi
(In *Anatomia de un Fracaso,*
    Introduction)
Santiago, Chile

1

The Only Alternative:
The Military Junta

The news of the fall of Allende and his government in Chile at the hands of a Military Junta of the nation was received in most quarters of the globe with sadness and with cries of foul play — everywhere, that is, except in Chile, where the majority of workers, farmers and lower middle-class groups, in spite of the fact that such a coup mortified them, received the news with an "it-was-bound-to-happen" attitude.

Practically all of the Chileans were, and still are, against a military coup; the majority of them, from seventy to eighty percent of the population, however, think that there was no other way to extricate the country from the situation it was in, except by an Army take-over.

If one asks any Chilean, of whatever political persuasion, at any geographical point in Chile, what he thinks of the military coup, his answer invariably is: "Well, look, I'm against military take-overs of political regimes, but things were so bad here that there was no other way out."

When a nation is as polarized as Chile was, when a country is on the verge of a bloody civil war, an arbiter has to step in. Most of the Chileans from all walks of life, from all political parties, even the leftist parties, except for fanatics, see and interpret the Army take-over as necessary and inevitable. The military coup came, I repeat, as a surprise everywhere in the world except in Chile. In fact many Chileans were surprised that it had not come earlier. The world was stunned because it had ideally put a halo around Allende's head. It imagined from without that the government of Allende was a government by the people and for the people. It had taken for granted that the Marxist government of Chile was a model of development which, in the future, would be adopted by the underdeveloped countries of the world.

The world, weary of the conservative bent of politics and of the injustices of the dominant economic class in Latin America, was used to the regular *opéra-bouffe* revolutions among the oligarchies and had grown indifferent to them. With the advent of Allende to the presidency of Chile, an interest for the whole of Latin America was rekindled in the world, in particular for Chile, and a new enthusiasm towards the person of Salvador Allende, the President of Chile, waxed forth. The world compared him to the great liberator of Latin America, Simón Bolívar, and saw in him a leader with the will to install a program of development and social justice which once and for all would help liberate Latin America from the shackles of poverty and misery existing since the Spanish Conquest.

The world, shaken out of its lethargy towards Latin America, enthused over the U.P. program, in part the product of its own imagination, and in part the result of an excellent public relations program in behalf of Allende's government, projected its own aspiration, desires and hopes for Latin America. The non-Chilean world did not even take time to examine closely to find out if the U.P. really corresponded to the image it had drawn of it. It presupposed that it did. It totally ignored the criticism of the U.P. regime made by Etienne Fajón, the editor of the Communist paper *L'Humanité* in France, and that of Graham Greene, the British novelist, sympathetic to the U.P. experiment.

(U.P. stands for *Unidad Popular,* i.e., Popular Unity. U.P. was the name given to the government of Allende. It was made up of the Socialist, Communist and MAPU political parties and two other small parties, the API and the Radical Party.)

The difference in perspective lay in that the world was looking at the political process in Chile from a distance and through a rosy prism. The Chileans, on the contrary, were being immersed in the experiment and they did not like what was happening to them.

The Allende government generated a class struggle and such a huge wave of envy and hatred among the Chileans that inevitably a civil war or a military coup was bound to arise.

At the level of the *poblaciones* (neighborhoods) which the U.P. controlled, a sort of political dictatorship was installed in which all kinds of means, good or bad, were used to further their end: church groups, labor unions, charitable organizations, social or recreational groups; lies, persecution and even physical violence. The government's unavowed but obvious intentions, typical of all Socialist countries, was to polarize society into two groups: fascists — *sediciosos* and *momios* — agents of external enemy forces on the one hand, and on the other, U.P. members, those who followed the party line, patriots, proletariats, the masses *(el pueblo)*. The Chileans were divided into the "bad guys," the bourgeoisie, and the "good guys," the poor.

For the U.P. there were no social problems but only subversive activities on the part of the opposition, fostered by imperialism. Nothing good could come from the opposition, even the most honest. The Communists in the U.P. believed that they, and only they, were the authentic representatives of the workers; that they alone possessed the truth; and that the members of the opposition were liars and imperialist "bastards." How could the opposition be right, when only the Communists possessed the truth? Since truth is indivisible, others could not pretend to it.

The Allende government on a human level had Stalinist overtones. It excelled to an incredible degree in character assassination through the news media of important political men of the opposition who were at variance with Marxist ideology. Smear tactics, psychological and other pressures of all kinds, sordid public campaigns of defamation in the press, radio and T.V., persecution of employees working in state-owned enterprises but affiliated to other parties, made up part of the arsenal used against Chileans who had the misfortune of independent thinking.

The class struggle in Chile, as in the other countries where it took place, was divisive in its very nature. It appears, however, that in Chile it generated more polarization, more hatred, than in any other country where it took place. Those engaged in battle against the bourgeoisie, the so-called oppressors, were themselves thinking and acting in terms of oppression. Their motivation was not based on more social justice for all, but on a corrosive envy of the rich. The class struggle was not conceptualized as an instrument whose ultimate finality, in spite of its transitory violence, was the formation of an integral community in which there were no more oppressors or oppressed.

Class struggle did not make a new man of the Chilean but a vindictive person bent on taking the place of the oppressor. The oppressed literally became in turn the oppressor. The class struggle in Chile was breeding a new kind of oppressor worse than the oppressor of yesterday. It was destroying the very fabric of the Chilean nation. The Communists were working night and day to form, organize and brainwash groups into closed subcultures and to inculcate in them hate and class division.

In Chile, fidelity to Marx was gauged by one's fidelity to Althusser, a French philosopher who was looked upon as the authentic contemporary interpreter of Marxism. In spite of the fact that he was more of a neopositivist than a Marxist, nevertheless, he was considered in Chile the high priest of the Marxist cult and ideology. The great weakness of Marxism in Chile, from a theoretical and a practical point of view, stemmed in great part from the importance that Chileans of the left, influenced by the works of Althusser, ascribed to Marxism as a scientific system, as a scientific interpretation of reality. Marxism is ruled out as an ideological, anthropological or philosophical system by Althusser. Marx, again in the opinion of Althusser, established his system on a purely scientific basis between 1845 and 1850, discarding at the same time the eschatological or philosophical notions that he might have had previously.

The interpretation of Althusser of Marxism as scientific, was accepted naively, uncritically, dogmatically. The social sciences were put on the same level as physical sciences. The logical consequence that followed was that a systematic scientific interpretation of social reality, if it is really as scientific as the interpretation of physical phenomena, became the only plausible, acceptable, conclusive interpretation. Since it is scientific it must be embraced. The solution it brought was imperative; the option it commanded allowed of no alternative. If an interpretation of the social reality and a political option based on this interpretation was scientific no other interpretation or political option was possible. In other words, Marxism was scientific and its interpretation of reality was scientific and infallible; therefore Communism was the only political system true to reality, scientific, and consequently in the name of science had to be imposed on all the people of Chile.

But the point is that in the domain of historical and social sciences there cannot be but one interpretation. If even in the physical sciences, interpretative scientific hypotheses succeed one another as knowledge of physical laws progresses, *a fortiori,* the same principle operates in social sciences. Marxism is one interpretation of reality, but not the only one, nor is it infallible.

In Chile, as mentioned, this uncritical acceptance of the stance of Althusser led to dogmatism, imposition of one interpretation of social reality, Manichaeism and one definite option. Those who did not accept the supposed scientific evidence of Marxism and Communism as the only plausible political system were looked upon as being outside of history, unscientific, obdurately old-fashioned, and closed to all that science and progress meant. In such a setting pluralism was impossible, as was openness of mind, reciprocal criticism, dialogue, choice of political options and commitments.

The supposedly "new man" of Socialism as an agent of social change simply did not exist. Nothing had changed in the clinics, dispensaries and hospitals of the National Health Services *(Servicio Nacional de Salud),* nor in the government offices, nor in the upper echelon of the *Empresas del Area Social* (government-run industries). In the offices of the diverse ministries of the government it was as it used to be, if not worse. Those left over from the other governments did not cooperate, it is true, but they were not given the example by the new members appointed by the U.P.

The leading social values that the U.P. desired to impose in Chile were not clearly set forth. No set of values, at least in practical fashion affecting the relationships between individuals outside production, were being inculcated in the masses. Public ownership was the only Socialistic element stressed. Much was said about political participation as being one of the most important elements in a Socialist society but in reality there was not more participation than there was before the U.P. came to power.

In Chile, as in other Socialist countries, the government made an all-out effort to be the sole employer. The ubiquitous U.P. was active in all industries, banks, commerce, and so on. The government almost had the monopoly of employment. That meant in practice the loss of political freedom. The fact that the government more and more was bent on being the sole employer and the fact that there were no institutional arrangements pertinent to the problem made it almost impossible for a person opposed to its policies to make a livelihood outside the government-controlled businesses.

There is no doubt at all that the U.P. had had considerable success in making drastic changes in the areas of industry, commerce and banking. Allende had broken the monopoly of economic power in the hands of the bourgeoisie. Unfortunately, Allende limited himself to changes in the economic sphere only and accomplished very little in the political and social spheres. The persons behind the political and social roles had changed, but the roles fundamentally had not. The social relationships, it is true, were not any more between the bourgeois industrial executive and the worker, nor between the *latifundista* (landowner) and the farmer, but this does not mean in any way that these relationships in their essence had been changed. The relationship existing in the social and the political were still those of domination and of dependence. The bourgeois-monopolized state had been replaced by an all-powerful bureaucratic dominating state, the capitalist technocrat by the state *interventor* (political appointee), and the once prosperous *latifundista* by the state agricultural engineer.

The system of social relations was based on centralization, vertical authoritarianism, lack of participation and as hierarchial as before. Only the persons in a position of authority had changed; the relations were still based on men at the top and men at the bottom; the relations still originated from above and flowed along one line, downward. No doubt, the government of the U.P. made an attempt to reorganize the system of social relations but it never considered seriously changing its essence. The same system which held sway under the bourgeoisie continued. True participation, historicity, political power on the part of the masses did not exist; and even worse, the U.P. had clearly no intention of bringing those changes about. Instinctively, the U.P., especially the Communist Party, were against the idea of giving the power directly or even indirectly to the masses.

In fact, the intermediary institutions between the government and the citizen, the unions, for example, had much less power during Allende's term than before. It was plainly the case for the C.U.T. *(Central Unica de Trabajadores,* Workers Central Union.) Before Allende's time the workers' unions had to be reckoned with in all spheres. With Allende, the unions became the lackeys of the government and lost all identity and independence. The policy of the government as regards participation, in spite of participation programs organized for the workers by the government in the state-owned industries, was clearly towards more and more centralization. In a letter dated July 30, 1973, one of his own ministers, the Minister of Health, Doctor Arturo Jirón, warned Allende: "The government talks a lot about democratization but does nothing to democratize. The government has big plans for decentralization, but there is no decentralization going on. There's a lot of big talk about participation, but there is [none] as yet. . . ."

Under the pretext that the U.P. was the government of the workers, of the people, the U.P. actually stripped the C.U.T., the S.U.T.E. (the teachers' union) of all effective political power. The unions and the workers were deprived in an effective manner of all power except the power against those opposed to the government. Their power was not a force within the government but a force against the forces opposed to the government. It was a power that the government made use of to protect itself, to protect its bureaucratic class. Neither the masses in general nor the unions participated in the government of the U.P.; they lacked an effective, positive, active role at all levels where decisions were being taken.

In the government of Allende, the masses were asked to participate in the defense of the government but not in the formation of a project for a better society or for the construction of Socialism. On the contrary, the government placed more and more obstacles in the carrying-out of political or economic projects on the part of the masses, of unions, of nongovernmental groupings, irrespective of whether or not these projects were favorable to the government. The role of the masses was essentially a role of guardianship, of defense of the government, of a sentinel in the night protecting from the subversive forces outside those within the government. In other words, the government of the U.P. maneuvered the masses outside history, outside active participation within the government.

The leaders, the "representatives" of the people decided the fate of those who were not there, of those who could have informed and illuminated the higher-ups in the government on their problems, their aspirations. Under the past government of the oligarchies, the workers were considered as instruments of production. Under Allende, the workers were used as watchmen to protect the new classes bred within the bureaucratic compounds. In all aspects, the social relations of the liberal capitalist government were in force; these had crystallized in other forms, but the constitutive elements of these forms were the same as before.

The economics of *Unidad Popular* cannot be evaluated for they were motivated exclusively by political strategy. By any economic criteria, its economic program was a failure. But since the criteria used for the implementing of its economic program were not economic but political, there is no point in making an economic criticism.

It might be useful, however, in general terms to note the high and the low points of the program. As mentioned before, nationalization was the most prominent development in the economic field; textiles, electronics, iron, copper, cement, nitrate along with the banks had been nationalized. On the one hand, in 1971 industrial output rose by 12.1%; wages increased not only relatively but also absolutely for the masses; unemployment decreased from 8.3% to 3.6%; consumption scored a great upsurge; and agrarian reform was speedily brought to its conclusion. On the other hand, in 1972, national production decreased by 4.5%; in 1973, by 10%; exchange reserves were extremely low; inflation the highest the country had ever known (163.4% in 1972, 500% in three years); employment more disguised than real; production decreased substantially in comparison to 1971; importation of equipment for industrial purposes had been curtailed drastically and the increase in imports was exclusively in foods.

Money reserves were practically nonexistent. According to Orlando Sáenz, "When the military government took over on September 11, there was in the Federal Reserve Bank of Chile *(Banco Central)* $3,500,000 — barely enough money to pay the necessary imports of one day."

The companies expropriated by the government turned into a fiasco. For example, after the government took over the telephone company even though the number of employees rose from 5,920 to 6,920, the growth of new services decreased. In 1970, the rate of increase of services was 13.12%; in 1971, 1.31%; in 1972, 2.41%. The company lost more than 3,000,000 escudos. The same was true for the SOQUIMICH (the nationalized nitrate companies); the number of employees rose from 9,800 to 12,000, but production slowed down.

According to Orlando Millas, Minister of Finance in Allende's government, "The 140 industrial companies taken over by the government lost fifty billion escudos in 1972. During the month of October, 1972, the government was obliged to print six billion escudos to make up for that month only the enormous deficit created by the state-owned companies." All this in the words of Millas "was due to the indiscipline of the workers, to the technical ignorance of the *interventores* (new managers named by the government to head the state-owned companies), to massive contracting of new personnel for political reasons, and to the extremely high salaries of the *interventores*." The quantity of money was tripled in respect to 1971 in order to finance the extremely high deficits of the companies taken over by the state and to cover the huge fiscal deficits incurred by these companies.

There were continued shortages of the most elementary products, such as bread. Meat was a luxury available four or five times a month. Housewives day in and day out had to stand in line for hours in order to get a meager ration of food for the day.

Corruption among the members of the government was rampant. Father Pablo Fontaine, a leading member of Priests for Socialism, in a letter dated February 11, 1973, to the Executive Secretary of the group, comments that the group is "systematically concealing the ambivalences of Marxism and the corruption among the parties of the government." The heads of the Chilean *Investigaciones* (similar to the FBI in the United States, Scotland Yard in England) were linked to Adolfo Sobosky and Joe Colombo of the American Mafia. For $30,000 a month they afforded protection to dope smugglers. They refused to collaborate with Interpol as in the case of the Chilean dentist, Iván Popic, who, at the time of his arrest by the Mexican police, had on his person twenty-two pounds of cocaine.

Many of the *interventores* used their posts for personal material advancement, amassing fortunes in black-market activities or simply expropriating the company's funds for themselves, as in the case of the *interventor* of the Los Chorillos mine.

Fifty automobiles and two of the most sumptu-

ous of the private residences of President Allende
were registered in the name of his private secretary,
Mirta Contreras Bell, better known as *La Payita*. According to a Canadian newspaper, the *Sunday
Express* of Ottawa, there had been deposited in her
personal name by the end of 1972, in one of the banks
of Ottawa, a sum of $6,000,000.

A Communist member of the House of Representatives for Valparaíso, Luis Guastavini, was found
with $145,000 in cash in a traveling bag he was carry-
ing as he was apprehended trying to flee the country
after the September coup.

The Chileans were incensed that key posts of
power decision were held by foreigners. The question
of whether it was for their good or not, they considered irrelevant. What was at stake was the principle
of self-determination, the right of the Chileans to decide for themselves — not Cuba nor Russia nor
foreign extremists — the course that their country
should take.

Law and order had ceased to function. Huge
land domains in the south of Chile were administra-
tively in the hands of *Miristas* (extremists). No one
was allowed to enter them without a recommen-
dation from an extremist. Terrorist groups, both of
the left (for example, the *Brigada Ramona Parra,*
made up of young Communist extremists), and of the
right *(Patria y Libertad),* with their firearms, chains,
swords, sharp-cutting weapons and lances, existed in
all the big cities. Clandestine organizations, such as
the International Brigade, ready on the spur of the
moment to launch an attack or instigate terrorist activities in all of the countries of South America, were
immune to law. The members of these organizations

served as instructors in the use of bombs, dynamite, firearms and guerrilla warfare.

The universities, whose student bodies had been swelled by thousands of political agitators, were no longer institutions of learning but places of political meetings, indoctrination, "conscientization," guerrilla training and formation of paramilitary groups. The police could not cope, or rather were not permitted to cope, with the mounting problems of violence and class warfare. I remember as I was riding on a bus from Talca to Santiago that a university student refused to pay his bus fare. The bus driver prudently said nothing, but at the first police headquarters on the highway stopped and reported what had happened. The police told him not to remonstrate but to simply go on his way. Their hands were tied; they could be demoted for making it hard for an extremist. The radical extremists during Allende's time were above the law.

In state-owned enterprises, lack of discipline was rampant. Some Belgian and Dutch priest-workers protested against the abuse of the workers and tried to impress upon them the principle that economic efficiency is also a basic social objective, but to no avail. Interminable coffee breaks, long lunch hours, recreational and rest periods, political meetings took up the time supposed to be spent working. They always had the same answer to anyone questioning their behavior: "We are the *dueños* (proprietors) now, and the *dueño* does not work."

2

On the Brink of Civil War

The Chileans were convinced that firearms were being smuggled to the extremists and that Allende, for all his lofty talk of legality and constitutionality, was at the same time encouraging the smuggling of arms and the setting up of guerrilla training centers.

The mystery of the contents of the much publicized wooden boxes sent from Cuba to President Allende came to light on September 11 when the list of the contents was discovered in the apartment of "Coco" Paredes, the chief, then, of the Federal Police. The voluminous cargo, on the orders of "Coco" Paredes and Hernan del Canto, the Minister of the Interior, had passed through customs without inspection. The opposition in Congress tried unsuccessfully to have a congressional committee investigate the matter. They claimed that the boxes contained arms. Allende said that they were replete with objects of art.

The list of arms found on September 11 proved beyond doubt that the opposition was right. The boxes contained firearms of all kinds.

S.I.M. (*Servicio de Inteligencia Militar,* Military Intelligence) had discovered evidence that massive clandestine importation of arms and ammunitions were in the hands of MIR (Revolutionary Movement of the Left), Altamirano's Socialist group and MAPU. There were arms everywhere: in hospitals, public ministries, banks, factories, the political head-quarters of the Socialist Party, in universities and in many other places.

A supervisor of camps built by the government for the summer vacations of the poor told me confidentially that they were used during the remaining nine months of the year as guerrilla training centers. To be frank, I didn't believe him, to such an extent that I did not even look into the matter to verify if what he said were true. It had become my habit — there were so many false rumors — of not admitting anything as true or false until I personally had verified it. I thought the idea of the use of summer camps for guerrilla centers, however, so preposterous that I did not even consider it worth investigating. But apparently, as it later turned out, what he said was true.

The extreme left and the extreme right rejected any dialogue whatever. Their main and only objective was confrontation. In a long radio speech, Altamirano, a member of the Senate and head of the Socialist Party to which President Allende belonged, solemnly declared that dialogue was impossible, and that it was not time for words but for action. In substance, this was also the position of MAPU and MIR. Altamirano and the head of MAPU, Oscar

Garreton, were charged with having incited the members of the Navy to mutiny. Whatever the merits of the case, one thing is certain — the extremists, i.e., MIR, MAPU, the Socialist faction of Altamirano, were out to divide the Armed Forces and neutralize them. MIR even put up posters on the walls of the principal cities of Chile, inciting the rank and file members of the Armed Forces to disobey their officers.

Developments in Chile were rushing to a denouement. It was inevitable. According to Etienne Fajón, editor of the Communist newspaper of Paris, France, *L'Humanité*, who had visited Chile a few days before the downfall of Allende, the errors of the government of the U.P. produced political polarization, economic chaos and the military take-over.

Fajón, in a press conference in Paris, blamed the overthrow of Allende on the stand taken by the Chilean left. "The seizing of industrial companies on the part of the workers," Fajón said, "is justified in an ulterior phase but not at the first phase of a change towards a socialistic society.

"Furthermore," he observed, "some firms were taken over, which in no way had ever been considered by the government as firms to be nationalized or socialized.

"The policy of remuneration," he went on, "did not take into consideration the legitimate interests of the technicians and engineers. . . .

"The publications of various organizations, especially MIR, encouraged unorthodox political positions and irresponsible concrete actions as, for example, the proclamations sent by the left to the soldiers urging them to disobey their superiors.

"This," he adds, "was of great importance in the decision taken by the Armed Forces to oust Allende.

"The importance given by MIR to the fact that workers alone should control the factories caused a strong rivalry between the workers on the one side and engineers, technicians and administrative personnel on the other."

Everybody in the country knew that Chile was on the verge of a civil war or of a military take-over. Any subject of conversation always turned to the fatal questions: When is the Army to intervene? When is the civil war going to begin?

Few letters going out of Chile failed to mention the chaotic situation which existed. For example, the Canadian Provincial of the Oblate Fathers in Santiago, in all of his letters in August, under one form or other, repeatedly said that the end was near, that it was a matter of weeks, that if Allende managed to find a workable solution to the crisis a special monument should be erected in his honor.

URGENT APPEALS OF THE CHURCHES

Time and time again the Catholic Bishops warned of the danger of civil war, of blood-spilling between brothers. Special prayers on many occasions were said to ward off the impending peril. On September 9, two days before the military take-over, an ecumenical service was held in Plaza de la Constitución, in Santiago, for peace. The faithful of all congregations were present — Lutherans, Baptists, Catholics, Jews, Methodists, Episcopalians and others.

The period of July 15-21, 1973, less than two

months before the military coup, was set aside as the week of prayers for peace. Religious services were held in all the churches. The object was to pray for peace in Chile. Here is the stated program of the week with its corresponding translation:

POR LA PAZ EN CHILE **O R A** **ANTE MARIA DEL CARMELO** **CON TU PARROQUIA:** 15-21 de Julio **CON TODA TU ZONA:** Av. Matta Domingo 22 de Julio A las 16 Hrs. (4 de la tarde) Proclamación de la Palabra de Dios, Celebración Eucarística **MADRE DEL CARMEN** **EN TI CONFIAMOS**	**FOR PEACE IN CHILE** **P R A Y** **TO OUR LADY** **OF MT. CARMEL** **WITH YOUR PARISH:** July 15-21 **WITH YOUR ZONE:** Ave. Matta Sunday, July 22 At 4 p.m. Proclamation of the Word of God Eucharistic Celebration **OUR LADY OF MT. CARMEL** **IN YOU WE** **PLACE OUR TRUST**

Time and again the Catholic bishops spoke of the dangers of civil war, of the need of dialogue between those on the left and those on the right. Here follows the list of their documents and some quotations:

LETTERS ON THE CRITICAL SITUATION EXISTING IN CHILE

April 1972 — Of Hope and Happiness (Message of the Bishops of Chile).

September 1972 — Tribulations and Hope (Message of the Cardinal of Santiago).

October 1972 — We Ask for a Constructive and Fraternal Spirit (Exhortation of the Bishops of Chile).

June 1973 — Only with Love Can a Country Be Built (Pastoral Letter of the Bishops of Central Chile).

July 1973 — Peace in Chile Has a Price (Exhortation of the Permanent Committee of Bishops).

The Church of Chile, anticipating the turn of events which took place in the country on September 11, had warned the political regime of Allende of its errors and had asked both the government and the opposition to come to a consensus as regards peace and social change.

"With this end in mind," the Church pointed out, "it was necessary that each side stopped trying to impose its social point of view as the only alternative solution."

The bishops asked that the nation put itself at the service of justice and not of violence or destruction: "Chile looks like a country scourged by war. We are greatly concerned with the black market. We grieve that so many professional people are leaving the country. We are much concerned with the media of communication which continually give false reports and by their monstrous campaigns of hate. . . . With sadness we observe day by day the mounting inflation and the impending crisis of our economy.

"On another occasion, in the name of the Church, we (the Bishops of Chile) declared: 'We are speaking in a dramatic moment for Chile. We don't represent any political party or group interest. We are concerned with the good of Chile; we are trying to prevent Christ's blood from being trampled upon in a fratricidal war. All of us Chileans are worried about the insistent news that civil populations are arming themselves, about the danger of a civil war. . . . Peace in Chile has a price. The price is a change of attitude, of mentality on the part of all of us. We fail to accomplish in the concrete, specific acts of justice. . . . Injustice leads to violence. The practice of justice produces the necessary conditions for peace. We humbly implore all the political and social entities to take the steps necessary to bring about a dialogue . . . ' " (Message of the Bishops of Chile, July 16, 1973).

Unfortunately this exhortation (of the bishops) and many other exhortations had no effect. As a reporter sympathetic to Allende's cause, remarked, "The alternatives were only two: a dictatorship in the name of the proletariat or in the name of the Armed Forces."

THE WARNINGS OF *MENSAJE*

Two editorials of *Mensaje*, a Jesuit monthly magazine with strong leanings to the left, one before the military coup and one after September 11, summarize very well the existing situation before the fall of Allende.

"A Santiago daily newspaper, in its edition of August 14, 1973, points out that 235 acts of terrorism have been perpetrated in the last two months. The list is growing day by day: dynamiting of towers of high-tension lines, of oil refineries, and the cruel death of two more victims. . . . Those against dialogue are the extremists of the right and of the left. They want confrontation at any cost. They exclude all dialogue; they don't seem to take into account the fact that sometimes it is necessary to compromise.

"The fact of the matter is that the extremists are totalitarians. They cannot share power. They want all the power for themselves. . . .

"The alternative is clear. Either dialogue or a bloody confrontation. . . . The U.P. must fight against the temptation of totalitarianism. They are at the most 44%, an important representation of the population, but nevertheless a minority" (*Mensaje,* No. 222, September 1973, p. 408).

The second editorial was written after the military coup:

"No political solution was forthcoming. The conversation between Christian Democrats and the government had come to an end. The unions were on strike indefinitely. Inflation was out of hand. The economic situation of the country was catastrophic. The country was almost paralyzed. There was no discipline among factory employees in their work. Administrative corruption was rampant. The extremists, armed to the teeth, openly proclaimed in an attempt to divide the Armed Forces that violence was the only solution.

"The first serious error of Allende was not to include the Christian Democrats in his government in order to broaden his political base.

"The other error, the most fundamental, was that Allende tried to play simultaneously on two levels; the level of legality, constitutionality, and the level of revolution, guerrillas and civil war. On the one hand, he always loftily proclaimed to all, again and again, that the Chilean way to Socialism was in accord with the legal principles existing in Chile and through constitutional means. On the other hand, influenced by Socialists and *Miristas,* he closed his eyes to the illegal shipment of arms being received by the extremists, to the guerrilla training camps and by direct action did his utmost to divide the Armed Forces" (*Mensaje,* No. 223, October 1973, pp. 468-469).

I repeat it once more. The outcome was not a surprise to most Chileans. What is surprising is that the Army waited such a long time before striking. The Army was reluctant to depose Allende for the following reasons:

1. The Chilean Army had a worldwide reputation as one of professional soldiers who traditionally stayed aloof from politics. Their respect and loyalty to the constitutionally appointed President was proverbial and served as an example and ideal to the other nations of Latin America. It is a well-known fact that on more than one occasion the Army desperately tried to save the government of Allende. If the Army had not entered the government at the time of the first transportation strike, it is very probable that Allende would have fallen then. It would not be exaggerated to say that on two occasions, thanks to the Armed Forces, Allende was able to remain in power.

2. The second reason is the political wizardry of President Allende himself. Anybody else but Allende would have capitulated months earlier. He was a consummate politician, who by his skill, versatility, en-

ergy and determination, time and again was able to stave off succeeding crises and to stay firm amid conflicting pressures.

However, time was running out for him. As crisis succeeded crisis in close succession, it was impossible for him not to falter. The military had joined the Cabinet twice in order to save him, but both times their efforts had been neutralized by extreme elements of the government. A third effort along these lines was judged by the military as useless. Only a coup could radically solve the situation. If Allende had restrained the extremists, he possibly would still be in power. But he could not; he was a prisoner of the machine he had built, if not by himself, at least built with his approval and knowledge.

3

The Blind Spot of the International Press

If all this is true, how can one explain the reaction of the worldwide press, its condemnation of the military coup and its passionate defense in behalf of Allende? How can one explain the legend built around Allende and his regime and propagated in all corners of the globe by the international press? What explanation can be given for the lack of objectivity, its notorious use of false reports?

Three reasons can be adduced: (1) Idealistic interpretation of reality based on wishful thinking and not on facts; (2) use of an antiquated framework of thought to analyze the Chilean reality; and (3) influence of Marxist propaganda.

1. *Idealistic interpretation of reality based on wishful thinking instead of on facts.*

As mentioned above, the world had placed great hopes in Allende. He was looked upon as the champion of the poor in Latin America, as another Simón Bolívar who would liberate the poor, this time not from Spain but from the inordinate rich, the international companies, and from the imperialism of the United States. What was visible to the world at large was Allende, the liberator, the man loyal to his word, to the law of the land, to the Constitution; what the world did not know, or did not want to know, or feigned not to know, were the machinations of Allende the *golpista,* the protector of the extremists, the fomentor in the background of the acts of violence, the guerrilla. The world press should have suspected something along this line, for after all, had he not been President of OLAS (Latin American Organization of Solidarity), an international movement of liberation by the use of violent and revolutionary means?

It was not asked if a man could go from one extreme to another overnight; from advocating the use of illegal, unconstitutional and violent means one day and the next day solemnly to be converted to the use of peaceful constitutional means. Apparently, it never dawned upon members of the international press that the use of legality by Allende could be a tactic to mask a long-term strategy of violence and cruelty which would erupt at the opportune and decisive moment.

Two reports on the Marxist experiment in Chile, one by Graham Greene of England, and the other by Etienne Fajón, the editor of *L'Humanité,* should have alerted the members of the international press to the fact that Allende's stewardship was not what they presumed it to be. But they completely ignored them. They preferred the flattering declarations of Francois

Mitterand who, upon his return to France, declared that the government of Allende, *Unidad Popular,* constituted a model which France should copy.

2. *Use of an antiquated framework of thought to interpret the Chilean reality.*

The categories used to analyze the Chilean reality were out of date. The country had changed, and so had the people. And this change was not in the direction that the international press had imagined it to be.

Many who belonged to the U.P. in 1971, or at least who were sympathetic to it, had changed their minds by 1972 and had gone over to the other camp. The newspaper reporters and political analysts interpreted the Chilean reality in static terms, along a continuum instead of in terms of discontinuity, change and setbacks. Their point of departure vitiated their view of the political spectrum, and in consequence their analysis of reality.

What initially and theoretically could have been a creative government in which the different groups pertaining to it could have guaranteed the free play of all the social forces, was in fact an uninspiring replica of the drab rigid Socialism of the other Socialist countries of the world. To say that the Chilean model of Socialism was new and different was to indulge in pure illusion. It was not original, specific to Chile, but conformed to the Socialist model known to all. The leftist Chilean only copied the Socialist model in its worst form, already obsolete.

The Marxist-Socialist government of Chile after two years and a half in office did not have much to show in its favor. Food was rationed, reserves were depleted, agriculture was stagnant, industrial growth from a boom high in 1971 was decreasing abnormally fast (beginning as of 1973); this from the economic point of view. From other points of view, the situation was even more serious. The country was divided between Quislings and patriots, between good and bad, U.P. and others. Hate, envy and rancor were rampant. The air was extremely charged. A spark could lead to a great explosion.

No doubt the government was not completely to blame for the sad state of affairs; on the international level, the government had difficulty in finding countries sympathetic to the new regime and willing to help. On the national level, the high bourgeois class had done, and was doing all it possibly could, to overthrow the government. All in all, however, fundamentally the state of affairs was due to the government. Unfortunately, the government did not want to assume its responsibility in the failure of the Socialist experiment. By blaming others for its shortcomings, it hoped by some devious way or other to stay in office and impose itself on the other fifty percent or sixty percent of the population inimical to it.

3. *Influence of Marxist propaganda.*

The international campaign against the Military Junta on the part of Russia and leftists throughout the world has had a noticeable influence on the reporting of the situation in Chile by the international press.

The Helsinki Communist Conference, of September 29 and 30, 1973, recognized "that the responsibility of the intense press and political campaign against the military government of Chile is due to the Soviet Union and its satellites headed by Cuba."

The resolutions affirm that "all kinds of pressures, political, diplomatic, etc., be used in order that foreign countries be prevailed upon to grant asylum to political refugees."

Yet it is common knowledge that from September 11, the majority of foreign embassies — France, Austria, Finland, Canada, Mexico, Honduras, Peru, Holland, Sweden, Argentina, Venezuela, Ecuador, Colombia, West Germany and Belgium — gave political asylum. No Socialist or Communist country except Cuba, which received one family, and Eastern Germany seventy-five persons, accepted political refugees.

The great majority, more than ninety-nine percent of political prisoners, although they all were of the left, had no desire of going to a Socialist or Communist country.

In the Center for Political Refugees under the auspices of Switzerland, the Director from Neuchatel, Switzerland, remarked that France, Holland and Switzerland had each admitted 300 political refugees with their families, of the thousand cases processed at the center, but that the Socialist and Communist countries had not accepted even one of the forty-eight refugees who had made application to be admitted in those countries.

In Helsinki, the Communists, choosing a political rather than humanitarian course, resolved to set up in every country a National Committee of Solidarity. In this manner they hope to capitalize on the reverses suffered in Chile, to depict the term of events in Chile not as a setback but as an urgent responsibility to solidarity of all the Communist countries in the world.

In the supposition that the world did not really

know what was going on inside Chile, that the metamorphosis in people's thinking between 1971-1973 eluded the world in general, and granting that the international press judged Allende's government in terms of wishful ideals, even though these suppositions had been discarded by the majority of Chileans — is it not true, one can ask, granting all that has just been said, that the international press has since September 11 had available objective information about what is really now taking place?

To see if it is so, to judge the objectivity of the international press since September 11, let us examine what has been written by it and compare it to the Chilean reality.

INTERNATIONAL PRESS REPORTS

The international press described Santiago as a city where thousands of people had been slain, where the streets were stained with blood, and in other similarly vivid terms.

The day after the siege of the Moneda (the Chilean White House) I walked downtown. I happened to live in the downtown section of Santiago, in which even then one could walk about freely, but which no one from the other sections of the city could enter for two days.

The downtown section was a sight sad to see. Bullets had pierced extra-thick windowpanes and chipped the walls of the State Bank and all the ministries and buildings in the immediate surroundings. The soldiers had engaged in a running gun battle with snipers during the day before. The relatively heavy fighting in Santiago, really the only battle areas, were at the Moneda between snipers and soldiers and at the State Technical University between students and troops. There was no fighting in other parts of Santiago except here and there sporadically between one or two snipers and military patrols. Nowhere in Santiago were the streets red with blood or filled with corpses.

Other reports emphasized that the resistance to the Army coup was massive. "Many thousands," claimed the press, "are reported killed and wounded in widespread resistance." These reports are absolutely false. There was no widespread resistance, not even token resistance, of any worth in all of Chile, except as mentioned at the Moneda and the State Technical University. In Concepción, the big industrial center, a beehive of extremist activities, where one could have presumed that heavy fighting would have taken place, not even a single shot was fired. Except for a few isolated cases of very small groups and of a few snipers, nowhere was there fighting in Santiago or in the rest of Chile.

The military coup was over by about four o'clock in the afternoon of the same day that it began. Even the military were surprised that no more resistance was offered on the part of the members of the U.P. They had estimated that the confrontation would last at least five days.

No one, practically speaking, except in the very few isolated cases mentioned, made an effort to defend the government. People were told to stay in their homes and workers were advised to return to their families in successive radio broadcasts by the military. The curfew was set at three p.m. on September

11. Ninety-nine point nine percent of the workers went back to their homes in obedience to the orders. A few went into hiding. As for the heads of the government, a few gave themselves up, but the majority of the others made a dash for the nearest embassy, leaving their followers to fend for themselves.

"More than 20,000 dead," proclaimed Radio Moscow and various foreign newspapers. "An army of 20,000 soldiers and paramilitary troops commanded by General Prats is marching from the south of Chile towards Santiago," another press report announced. Absolutely false! There was no organized or prolonged resistance of any kind, I repeat, in all of Chile. Stories of massive confrontation, napalm attacks, and the like, are ridiculously false. One foreign press report claimed, "The Sumar factory was completely destroyed. A terrible battle took place in which 500 workers were killed." False. The Sumar factory and all other factories, as far as that goes, are standing with not even a scar. The workers in general are all there working harder than they did during the previous three years. There are bullet marks on some of the factories but these date back to skirmishes between police or military with armed workers before September 11.

When I say there was no resistance, practically speaking, against the Junta, I want in no way to imply that there will not be any. The extremist movement, MIR, is completely intact. Only about forty percent of the arms smuggled into Chile have been found. Any day terrorist acts can begin, guerrilla tactics can break out. What I want to make clear is that contrary to what the press said in general, there was no substantial resistance of any kind.

Rumors and an incredible number of tales circulated in Santiago, especially the first three weeks after the military coup. The stories of repression, atrocities, mass executions and tortures were endless. As time goes by, however, more and more rumors are proved not to be true. For example, I had been asked to participate in a Funeral Mass for Father Juan Brinkoff, a Dutch priest, supposedly killed by the military. The news had first come from the Chancery of the Archdiocese of Santiago which had been notified by the Nuncio of the Vatican. The Embassy of Holland had confirmed the news. A few hours before the scheduled Mass, news came from the Dutch Embassy that Father Brinkoff probably was not dead. In fact, two days later the definite news came that he was alive and well. Today he is in Holland doing pastoral work.

On another occasion a Belgian nun from Concepción reported that a Socialist, the president of a Catholic labor movement, had fled to Argentina and that his family had joined him. The fact of the matter is that neither he nor his family had fled.

Rumors prevailed that an incredible number of people from the poor districts of Santiago had been killed by the military. About ninety-eight percent of these "dead" persons are back in their *poblaciones* and alive. They had gone into hiding or had been arrested and brought to the National Stadium. *Newsweek* claimed, "With hardly an exception the victims came from the *poblaciones,* the slums that encircle Santiago." I investigated the following eleven slum districts (the number in parentheses refers to the total dead from the *población* from the outbreak of the coup on September 11 through October 15): La

Palma (0); Nogales (3 or 4); 6 de Mayo (2); Pablo de Roca (2); La Legua (10); Población Kennedy (3); San Rafael (4); Santa Cristina (4); Barrancas (10); San Gregorio (6); San Miguel (8).

Rumors had it that 600 students had been slain at the Technical University in Santiago. One student, an extremist, who was there when the battle took place, told me that there had been sixty fatal casualties — a tragically high number but hardly the total of the rumors.

As for the city morgue, reported to be filled, that in itself should have been no surprise. It is always filled. There were more bodies than usual but as a worker said, many of the bodies were not claimed for days and days. It is not easy to get at the truth. What is deplorable, however, is that rumors were reported as facts, sources quoted without checking, witnesses accepted as unimpeachable without an examination of their credentials.

I do not affirm that there were no tortures, no killings. There were. What I claim is that they were grossly exaggerated. The consequence is that today the reports on Chile are dismissed as propaganda. Tortures and murders are still going on, but unfortunately people do not believe any more the reports of such activities. They were fed so many false reports by the international press that they now are wary of being "taken" again.

4

The United States and the Downfall of Allende

Many commentators, directly or indirectly, lay the blame of Allende's downfall on the United States. For example, the Chilean Communist Party says that the coup against Allende was directed by the American government and business enterprises. (In this, the Chilean Communists follow the official party line dictated by Moscow, but privately they angrily and exclusively blame the extremists of the left, i.e., MIR, MAPU and the left wing of the Socialist Party for the downfall of Allende.) This is the propaganda used by the majority of Communist and Socialist countries in their endeavor to discredit the present Military Junta and to convince the world of the nefarious role that the United States plays in Latin America. However, not only Communist countries and Communist cadres think that the United States played a major role in Allende's downfall. Many academicians and political analysts in the United States, certain members of the American government, newspaper reporters and a good percentage of the public at large harbor the same thoughts regarding the undercover role of the United States.

The United States is blamed either (a) directly, (b) indirectly, or (c) by default, for the abrupt end of Allende's regime in Chile.

(a) *Directly.* Some claim that the American government was directly involved in the coup and that it never would have happened without the direct aid and covert infiltration of the United States in the Chilean Army. The actual facts seem to point otherwise. The Military Junta did not ask American help, and didn't need it. The coup was strictly a decision taken by the Army alone and backed by the majority of the population. The United States was in no way directly involved in the action of the Military Junta.

The arguments used to prove that the United States was directly involved, that the American government was sympathetic to a coup, that the United States knew of it beforehand, do not prove in any way that America was directly involved. Those who believe that the United States was directly involved marshal past historical facts to prove their point. They mention previous direct interventions on the part of the United States and in particular the more recent ITT intervention in Chile. While it can be accepted that the American government or American companies were involved in certain events in the past, these facts do not prove in any way that this was the case in the recent military coup.

(b) *Indirectly.* Others, while conceding that the United States was not directly involved, still blame the American government indirectly for Allende's downfall. They claim that the economic policies of the United States indirectly set the stage for the demise of the U.P. There is no doubt that indirectly, on an economic level, America did play a role. However, this role was not a prominent one nor an important one. It was but one of other minor factors, not in any way a major one, which contributed to Allende's demise. It is claimed that the curtailment by the United States of all credits to the Allende government, the blocking of loans by international financial institutions, and the stopping of all economic programs excepting those related to the Chilean Armed Forces, indirectly precipitated the crisis.

It is true that the United States stopped all credits but these were more than offset by credits from other countries. Allende received more credit in his three years of office than any other President of Chile. Chile received credits from Argentina, Brazil, Peru, Mexico, France, Finland, Holland, USSR, China, Poland, Bulgaria, Hungary, Rumania, Czechoslovakia, East Germany, West Germany, Sweden and North Korea. Chile's total external debt rose from 2,446 million dollars at the end of 1970 to 2,992 million at the end of 1972, almost a million a day.

The lack of American credit was not an indirect cause of the failure of Allende's government, for the credits from other countries more than made up for the credits denied him by the United States. The blame is to be laid exclusively to the economic policies of Allende. The fact that other countries supplied credits equivalent to or superior to credits of the American government proves that the lack of credits on the part of the United States did not play the role

attributed to it by critics of American economic policies towards Allende. With or without credits, the
economy of the country was in extremely serious
trouble. The serious problem of the Chilean economy
was due to internal mismanagement; economic criteria did not exist because political criteria had sup-
planted them.

(c) *By default*. In a conversation with Representative Michael F. Harrington, a member of the American Congress, at the home of the representative of the
Columbia Broadcasting System, I was asked if A-
llende would have remained in power had the United
States cooperated more than it did. "In the short run
he probably would have survived longer," I an-
swered, "but in the long run, he was doomed."

Things fundamentally could not have changed,
unless Allende and his followers would have changed
themselves. Even if the United States had cooperated
to the fullest extent possible (this is equally true for
the Church, the Christian Democrat Party, and many
others), it is very improbable that the government of
Allende would have survived much longer than it did.
The only way Allende could have survived was to
broaden his base and mend his economic and political errors. His fervor for Marxism was the fervor of a
neophyte. His political strategy was not based on the
Chilean reality but was the result of *a priori* Marxist
ideology divorced from reality. He made abstraction
of the large middle class, of the political "conscientization" of the Chileans. Spurred on by extremists of
MAPU, the Socialist Party and MIR, Allende's main
objective was the dictatorship of the proletariat.
Sooner or later the Chileans were bound to object
and overthrow him.

The indirect role played by the American government in Allende's downfall on the economic level is much less debatable than its role on the political level. The CIA, presumably acting upon orders from the White House, spent three million dollars prior to Allende's election in an effort to defeat him and some eight million in clandestine operations to topple him once elected. Without doubt the United States did play a role — minimal, insignificant, inconsequential, be that as it may — but nevertheless a role in the downfall of Allende. It was not in its long-term interest to assume such a role.

As S. Kubisch, Assistant Secretary of State for Latin-American Affairs, says: "It was not in our interest to have the military take over in Chile. It would have been better had Allende served his entire term taking the nation and the Chilean people into complete and total ruin. Only then would people have gotten the message that Socialism doesn't work. What has happened has confused this lesson."

It is not defensible either. Referring to Chile, Secretary of State Henry Kissinger is reported to have said, "I don't see why we should have to stand by and let a country go Communist due to the irresponsibility of its own people." If he did say this, he is mistaken. By the same token, Russia could interfere in American politics on the pretext that people who passively accept to be ruled by a President and a Vice President not elected by the people are immature.

The United States had no business interfering in Chilean internal affairs; neither for that matter did Russia, North Korea, North Vietnam or Cuba. Small countries have as much right to decide their future as the big countries.

To say that the United States had no right to interfere in the internal affairs of Chile does not mean, however, that American actions had a causal *de facto* relationship, even if indirect, in Allende's being overthrown. The truth of the matter is that what happened would have happened, irrespective of the American position. Even if the United States had not participated in any way, whatsoever, even if it had been behind him to the hilt, Allende would not have remained as President of Chile. The revolt was an internal revolt by the majority of the Chileans against Allende. In no way in the total analysis is the United States responsible for his ouster.

The events of September 11 were the logical outcome of the social, economic and political policies of Allende. The responsibility for what took place lies with Salvador Allende — he more than anyone else is responsible for what happened on September 11. It is true that *Patria y Libertad,* an organization of the extreme right and MIR, an organization of the extreme left; Tieme, head of *Patria y Libertad,* and Altamirano, the leader of the left wing of the Socialist Party; the reactionary members of *Partido Nacional* and MAPU, and the Communists have a great responsibility in the debacle as do the Christian Democrats, in a lesser degree.

In any balance sheet, all the Chileans collectively are to blame, but in the final analysis the responsibility for the outcome is to be attributed not to MIR nor *Patria y Libertad,* nor the Christian Democrat party, nor Altamirano, nor MAPU, nor the CIA, nor Cuba, nor Russia, but fundamentally to Allende himself. Unfortunately, the press does not want to admit this. But facts are facts. They can be ignored, denied, but cannot be changed. To repeat what I said, what happened on September 11 was the logical and necessary outcome of a social, political and economic process dependent on Allende.

THE MYTH OF ALLENDE'S MAJORITY

It has been, and is still being claimed, that the fall of Allende was the end of democracy in Chile, that the coup was instigated by the rich against the vast majority of Chileans who sided with Allende. Those who defend this position presume that the majority of Chileans were in favor of Allende.

Chile is presented, during the time of Allende, as a country divided politically between a minority of rich people in opposition to and a vast majority in favor of Allende. However, factually, the reality was quite different. Allende in the presidential election received 36.2% of the total votes cast; in the municipal elections of April 1971, his political coalition received between 49.9% and 50.1%; and in the parliamentary elections of March 1973, between 43% and 44%, according to the official figures released by the government. The figures of the March elections have been vigorously contested. A commission of the Law School of the Catholic University, with their own computers (they had in the past presidential and municipal elections approximated the same number as the official count), claimed that 65% of the total votes were cast for the opposition, and only 35% for the government.

An inquiry is going on at the time of this writing. It is claimed that over 300,000 multiple enrollments in favor of the U.P. have been discovered. Whatever the result of this investigation, one thing is clear: in Santiago, in the last parliamentary elections, in districts in which the opposition had a clear advantage, all kinds of obstructions were placed by the government to make voting difficult if not impossible, especially for women. Women were, as is generally known, against the Allende government. Delaying tactics of all sorts were used. For example, a person in favor of the U.P. would use up as much time as possible to cast his vote. The result was that long lines formed, and women had to stand five to six hours in line before being able to cast their votes before the closing time of the polls.

It was plain to anyone living in Chile that Allende's popularity was rapidly eroding, even among his most ardent followers. For example, the former President, Eduardo Frei, running for senator in the Quinta Normal district, one of the largest of the poor suburbs of Santiago, overwhelmingly in favor of the U.P. and Allende in the presidential and municipal elections, won easily by a large margin over his government opponents.

The huge numbers of people at political gatherings for the U.P. and Allende are put forward as evident proof that his followers numbered more than a million. It is true that the political demonstrations in support of Allende were in general huge, except the last one, on the third anniversary of his election as President, which numbered less than 100,000 (not 800,000 as has been said in the international press). But not all these people were for Allende, far from it. It must not be forgotten that attendance was obligatory for the workers of state enterprises.

They were dismissed from three to six hours before the event with the understanding that the time off from work had to be made up by attendance at political rallies. Those who failed to attend them were severely reprimanded and even dismissed. Workers from cities and towns, sometimes a hundred miles from Santiago, were herded into buses and trains to swell the number. People, decidedly not in favor of Allende, would come to Santiago from cities as far away as Concepción, about 350 miles distant, and visit with relatives, taking advantage of a free round trip offered to those willing to participate in a political demonstration in favor of Allende.

The majority of the Chileans by 1973 were not for Allende. It is true that for a very short period, Allende's forces in the municipal elections of 1971 achieved or came close to a majority. In fact, they probably had the majority, between 49.9% and 50.1% of the votes cast. As early, however, as 1972 the tide began to turn against him, gradually ebbing in 1973 to a very low mark. Allende and the U.P. were very much aware of this. That is why Allende always refused to call for a plebiscite. A plebiscite would have been the best democratic means at his disposal of knowing exactly where he stood with his people, and his people with him. A plebiscite, a means provided for by the Constitution, to break a stalemate in a democratic way, would have decided once and for all where the country stood.

Allende never dared use it; he, as well as everybody else in Chile, knew beforehand that the outcome would be unfavorable to him. Furthermore, one must keep in mind that at heart Allende was not democratic but a disciple of Lenin. His final objective was to take power, one way or another, and impose his will upon the people. What mattered, in his mind, was not what the people wanted, but what he wanted for the people. His conception of democracy smacked of authoritarianism, despotism, paternalism. The military coup was more democratic than it may appear at first sight, for it rested fundamentally on the mandate of the majority of the people of Chile.

A correspondent from Concepción wrote to an American newspaper: "Radical reformation by democratic means is not impossible; what is impossible is the transformation of a democracy into a totalitarian one by democracy. Allende knew well that the Marxist state he was aiming at could not be achieved by democratic means. He pretended otherwise, but in actual fact what he was up to was to gain a position of power from which he might launch a final violent attack."

5

Priests — Between Allende and the Armed Forces

Regarding the clergy of Chile, three questions are often asked. Is it true that priests were divided on the issue of Socialism? Is it true that many foreign priests had to leave Chile after the military coup? Were foreign priests for the most part in favor of Allende? The answer is affirmative in all three cases.

The priests, reflecting the extreme polarization of the populace, were in general either to the left or to the right. More than 125 foreign missionary priests left Chile after September 11. This number includes those who were ordered out of the country, those who sought political asylum in embassies and those who left voluntarily but who probably would have had to leave if they had stayed in Chile.

Many of these priests were Marxists, not on a theoretical or philosophical level, but on a pragmatic, political level. In general they were in favor of the use of violent means (guerrilla tactics, civil war, revolution) rather than dialogue. Most were deeply engaged in politics, not in the general sense of the word but in the partisan sense of the word.

Many priests faced with the immense injustices rampant in Chile had adopted Marxism as a tool to liberate people because they saw in Marxism the only plausible means of effectively and efficiently making the necessary socioeconomic changes, and had accepted Socialism because of the values of equality, fraternity and solidarity which Socialism on a practical level invoked in their minds.

They claimed that commitment to liberation of the masses from misery and underdevelopment was a greater proof of faith than commitment to the Church. The criterion of faith was reduced to socioeconomic and political action. They were apostles not of salvation but of Marxism and Socialism. They imagined that the Kingdom of God in Latin America could come about through the doctrine of Marx. They operated almost exclusively on a horizontal level. The vertical level had been postponed if not abandoned. On a practical level, politics had replaced faith; the political party, the Church; utopia, eschatology; political concentrations and public demonstrations, cult and liturgy.

Their faith in politics and political parties was absolute; their absolute faith in God had been made relative. Faith had become an ideology, liberation had been reduced to its social dimension, politics had become the supreme value of their lives, the kingdom of heaven had been replaced by the kingdom of the earth, and eschatology had become humanistic utopia.

In judging the action of the Armed Forces as regards these priests, one must bear in mind the fact that they had entered Chile under the expressed reservation stipulated by the government that they would not take part in political activities during their stay in Chile. The Church likewise on numerous occasions had enjoined them not to take part in politics and condemned more than once the role assumed by priests in political parties. For example, the letter of the Bishops of Chile to the twelve priests from Chile who had gone to Cuba and written a public letter with a profound political bias, states, "As for foreign-born priests, we ask them to remember that they are not in their own country, and consequently should be extremely careful in their judgments of a political nature. We greatly appreciate the services that they render to the Church of Chile but we caution them as we do the Chilean-born priests, and in this case even more strongly, not to engage in party politics."

The accusation that the Chilean people, in general, voice against the role played by foreign-born priests in Chilean politics is that as outsiders they had no right to try to impose upon Chileans their political views. Chileans themselves wanted to decide under what system — political, economic, social — they chose to live without interference of foreign-born priests. Their rejection of foreign influence on their national lives included other Allende-imported foreigners of the left. As many a Chilean asked, "How would Americans react if we Chileans went to your country and told you how to vote or reorganize your government? You would not like it. Neither do we."

The principle of self-determination which the Chileans invoke, that is, the inalienable right of the

Chileans themselves, without any interference from people from other countries, to determine their political affairs is a basic principle of the Charter of Human Rights.

If a foreign missioner wants to go into politics he may do one of two things: Either return to his native country to take part in its political affairs or make out an application to return as an immigrant, not as a priest, to the foreign country he was working in. If he is accepted for citizenship, he will be able to give himself entirely to politics. His life will not be different in many instances, politically speaking, from what it was before. His role, however, will not be criticized by the citizens of the country in question. The same applies to his role as regards the faithful. He will not present himself as a priest trying to steer them into a political party, to impose a political option in the name of the Church from the pulpit but as an ordinary citizen free to engage in political activities.

The fact that there was in Chile a tremendous social disparity plus a great need for many changes in the economic, political and social fields helps one to understand how a priest living with the poor and sharing their burdens came to mix religion with partisan politics. He acted from zeal but imprudently. He failed to understand that in the Chilean view it is not up to foreign missioners to introduce these changes through party politics; it is up to the Chileans themselves, exclusively. Besides, it is only common sense not to get involved as strangers in politics in Chile which even the Chileans themselves find extremely complex, vaporous and difficult.

It is inconceivable that priests (for example, some missionary priests from Holland, two or three months after their arrival) tried to impose upon the Chilean people among whom they worked their own political, economic, cultural and religious creed. Instead of submitting to a process of Chilean acculturation, they imposed on Chileans a process of Dutch acculturation with their own goals and idiosyncracies. They were virulent in their denunciation of Yankee imperialism but did not notice that they themselves were doing the very same thing of which they were accusing Americans.

In general, the foreign priests who sided with Allende and engaged in party politics were very dogmatic. They would not dialogue nor would they accept that others could offer different solutions. Those who did not conform to their own thinking were regarded as reactionaries. Automatically they closed the door of argument on other solutions besides the Marxist one and they categorically refused to even consider other possibilities. They could not tolerate criticism against the U.P. by others even when the criticism was positive. All that the U.P. did, merited, in their eyes, the strongest approbation. They were completely acritical of Allende and his government.

If the organization of Priests for Socialism had commended Allende when it was appropriate and criticized him when it was necessary, perhaps they would have helped him steer another course. But unfortunately, they were so fanatical and dogmatic in their approach that they believed that outside the U.P. nothing good could exist. They lacked a sense of history and jumped into utopia.

Ironically, today it is the priests of the right who are guilty of the same type of behavior. For them the military government is the answer to the prayers of the Chileans. It can do no harm whatsoever. Tortures and killings they accept as a necessary evil. They are as fanatical as those of the left were in Allende's time. They seem to forget that their attitude towards the present Military Junta could be as detrimental as was that of the Priests for Socialism in behalf of Allende. They are closed, dogmatic, clerical. They, too, reject all other solutions but their own canonization of the Junta.

As those of the left, they look at the Chilean reality with one pair of glasses and refuse to even try another pair for fear that they might see a different reality. If the evangelization of the priest of the left was more political than evangelical at least there was an interest in the promotion of the poor on the material level. The priest of the right today is not evangelical but clerical, disincarnate; his perspective is that of the bourgeois. The poor and the suffering are, as it were, outside his fold.

The priests of the right during Allende's period were outside of history; today they think they are in history but they are not. They do not realize that they have sacrificed the essential ministry of their calling — evangelizing the poor. They seem not to be disturbed by the fact that there are tortures and killings, that thousands of people are out of work simply because they belonged to political parties of the left; that thousands of students find university doors closed, many with their courses of study practically finished — students of medicine, engineering, law, sociology, electronics, and so on — because they belonged to the political parties at the helm during Allende's regime. They appear not to be disturbed that thousands suffer hunger, persecution and poverty.

Bishop Gilmore, the Vicar of the Armed Forces, and many of the military chaplains are a case in point. It is their duty, and it is especially the duty of Bishop Gilmore, to warn their pastoral charges, the Armed Forces, against the cruel tortures, killings, imprisonment and dismissal from work which are being inflicted upon the Chileans. Unhappily, they are shirking their official duty. They have not lifted their voices in favor of the poor; on the contrary they are taking sides with the military. They are with the rich, the oppressors; they are against the poor, the persecuted.

Jaime Guzman, lawyer, brilliant polemist, a practicing Catholic, is another case in point. He more than anyone else spoke up against abuses in the U.P. government. By his long, patient investigation of the manipulations of the bureaucrats of the U.P., by his dedication to the safeguard of human rights, he was able to expose in an objective, detached manner the machinations of the U.P. Today, however, not only does he maintain silence on the subject of tortures, killings, abject poverty and untold sufferings of the poor, but even refuses to pry below the surface of reality to see if these charges are true. He is so convinced that the Armed Forces can do no harm that he dismisses in a superficial manner reports to the contrary. Whether he realizes it or not, he has turned his back on the poor, the persecuted, the suffering. From a champion for the rights of the human person during Allende's administration he has become, in good faith, the champion of oppressors and persecutors.

These two cases reflect in great part the image of those of the right in the Church today in Chile. Father Hasbun, the former director of the television

Salvador Allende speaks to Chile's copper miners following nationalization.

Allende enters Santiago Cathedral with Cardinal Raul Silva Henriquez. In the beginning of the Allende regime, the Church worked closely with the government.

One of Allende's constant charges was that of outside influence on Chile. Observers often used ITT as an example of such influence.

Father Paul Hasbun, director of television channel 13 in Santiago, was a strong critic of the Allende regime and Unidad Popular. He was later fired by the Military Junta.

President Allende is shown greeting a group called Christians for Socialism. To the President's right is a bishop who was a member of the group which held that Catholicism and Marxism could work out an accommodation. Others to Allende's left are priests.

Late in his regime, the women of Chile turned against Allende, taking to the streets, hammering on pots and pans. It was called the "Battle of the Pots."

Military authorities in Chile claimed this revolutionary statue was found in a left-wing guerrilla hideout in southern Chile.

A nationwide truck strike helped bring about Allende's downfall. Here, hundreds of trucks are parked in a San-tiago suburb.

Soldiers point their weapons toward the presidential palace during the 1973 military take-over.

This shows the destruction of the presidential palace during the take-over.

Chilean soldiers burn Marxist literature in Santiago.

Antitank missiles form part of an arsenal found at the Tomas Moro presidential summer residence, also used as a guerrilla training center.

Plan - Prov. de Santiago (invierno)

Imp. :- Pruin - Inf. la Bda - Tacher - Blendados N° 2.

mp :- Esc. a heliptuls - Ferrocarriles Pta alta - Telecomunicaciones
Ing. Tup Viadus (material) - Fach - El Bosque, mp> 10 - Carabineros
(ser. ap kd Bup)

unidades no euplatos . (otras)

Hipótesis - Felipe mantiene
contacto con 1 unidad FF.AA aptuluns Pruin-Tocna.
q' cops estos en juego - (ha huelo)
enemigo - ataque Ra-cudo N° 2 - Ese. inf. la Bda.
juego vide (2 alt.)

① ayuje a mas retan insurpt
kuja banco alta al aire

② ayuje lega uno, team mens
infumucion couticauida. tapa el
aire - stala linea a comunicacion.

This document, seized after the Allende overthrow, is said to be a plan of attack by Allende forces for the city of Santiago.

P R O G R A M A

PREPARACION TACTICA DE LA GUARNICION DE "TOMAS MORO"

SECCION I

TEMAS Y CALCULO DE HORAS

No. Tema	Nombre	Tiempo
1	Generalidades del combate en la ciudad	3 horas
2	El combatiente en la ofensiva en la -- ciudad	3 horas
3	El combatiente en la defensa en la ciudad	3 horas
4	El Grupo Operativo (Escuadra) en la ofensiva en la ciudad	9 horas
5	El Grupo Operativo (Escuadra)en la defensa en la ciudad	12 horas
6	La Fuerza Operativa en la defensa de un Objetivo	12 horas
		42 horas

A copy of the guerrilla curriculum at the Tomas Moro presidential summer residence.

*Members of the Military Junta consult Cardinal Raul
Silva Henriquez of Santiago.*

Chile's ruling Junta presides during a celebration marking the six-month anniversary of its coming to power. Former President Eduardo Frey declined an invitation to attend.

After the Allende overthrow, the Armed Forces had all traces of his regime removed. Here workers wash down a wall which had contained slogans supporting Allende.

The first contingent of refugees from Chile to be granted permission to enter Switzerland arrives in Geneva.

channel of the Catholic University of Chile, is an example of a new trend, however small, among those of the right.

In his forthright and energetic condemnations of the abuses of the U.P. government, in his defense of human rights, he was looked upon by the right as the dauntless champion of the persecuted. He welcomed with open arms the Military Junta. It took some time for him to realize what the military were up to but when he did he had the courage to speak out against them. He rediscovered the charisma of evangelization to the poor in the face of the injustice and the arbitrariness of the military.

6

Plan Zeta

What about Plan Zeta? Supposedly this secret plan contained the details of the operations for a complete seizing of political power in Chile by the forces of the U.P. Its main thrust was the formation of a people's government modeled on Russia and Cuba. It explicitly did away with the opposition — the rich, the officers of the Armed Forces and their wives and children, and the political leaders of the opposition. All those against the U.P. regime were to be inexorably murdered.

According to the Military Junta the existence of Plan Zeta is absolute and certain. The Junta claims to have found the preamble to it in the *Banco Central de Chile* (Federal Reserve Bank). Here are excerpts from both the preamble and the plan as outlined. Full details are contained in the Junta's White Paper.

The preamble to Plan Zeta as revealed in the

documents, part handwritten and part typewritten, is as follows:

1. Organize a high strategic command composed of Salvador Allende, Carlos Altamirano, Luis Corvalán, Oscar Garreton, Luis Orlandini, and possibly Eduardo Nova.

2. Organize and train members of the U.P. for paramilitary operations.

3. Draw up a mode of action whose main characteristic would consist in flexibility.

4. Set up meeting points and centers in industries, union halls and political party headquarters to prepare for and carry out the plan promptly at a moment's notice.

5. Execute all local military, police, judicial and administrative heads, and all the high-ranking members of the opposition.

6. Seize control of all land, sea and air transportation, railroad stations and airports.

7. Take control of the communications system: telephone, telegraph and international news agencies.

8. Occupy radio stations, television channels, newspapers and magazines in order to: (a) deprive the opposition of the use of them and (b) use these media to "conscientize" the masses and to give them the signal for the last frontal attack.

PLAN ZETA FOR CONCEPCIÓN

The details of Plan Zeta for the city of Concepción were reportedly discovered in secret documents found together with weapons in the attic of the headquarters of the Socialist Party at 46 Castellon Street,

Concepción. In a briefcase belonging to Rafael Merino Hernández, professor of philosophy at the University of Concepción and regional secretary of the Socialist Party, was found a notebook listing alphabetically the names of 600 men from Concepción who together with their wives and children were to be shot on September 17.

Some were to be murdered at their work, others at home. The mixed commando groups (young girls and young men) were made up of Socialists and *Miristas*. The authorities and administrative officials of the University of Concepción who were opposed to *Unidad Popular* were to be disposed of by the feminine members of the commando groups. The list contained the names of all the military officers of the Third Army Division Headquarters in Concepción together with their wives and children, the officers in charge of the garrison units of the city, the ministers of the Appellate Court, several judges, the names of all the members of the Regional Council of Professionals, several newspaper reporters, political leaders of the opposition and varied professionals.

PLAN ZETA FOR ARICA

Plan Zeta for Arica plotted in Antofagasta reached Arica about the middle of August 1973. Immediately the key posts in the plan were filled by local people and groups were named for specific functions. Already some of these groups were operating as, for example, the group in charge of arms and explosives.

The cold decision to massacre thousands of officers and soldiers is attested to by the instructions given in the plan for the operation of September 17 against the Armed Forces throughout the country when they were to hold their final dress rehearsal of the military parade for the following day, September 18, National Independence Day. This final practice regularly takes place in the presence of military authorities. The public stands on the left of the marching soldiers, facing the reviewing stand. The strategy of Plan Zeta consisted in planting among the public hundreds of armed individuals who would fire at the officers and soldiers as they were marching "eyes right" before the reviewing stand. In the ensuing confusion and panic they hoped that they would have time to flee and that the troops would not shoot blindly at the crowd.

In a support operation while this was taking place, large crowds of women and children were supposed to approach and penetrate into the headquarters of the military and police forces in the city, imploring the guards not to shoot.

This maneuver, it was thought, would neutralize the soldiers and the policemen. All during this time, other groups would take possession and control of public utilities, industries and points of access to the city. Other groups would strike at and murder well-known personalities opposed to Allende.

DID PLAN ZETA EXIST?

Plan Zeta probably did exist but it has not yet been absolutely proven that it did. There is evidence that corroborates the existence of plans to take over the government and get rid of all who were opposed to it or presumed to be against the eventual new government. But to pinpoint any plan and say definitely that this was Plan Zeta is another story.

That a plan was being drawn up and seriously studied is very probable from evidence at hand. That there was a plan definitely finalized with the exact date of its execution and that it had been approved and decided upon by all the political factions of *Unidad Popular* is not at all clear. The political parties which made up the U.P. undoubtedly discussed the problem of armed confrontation, insurrection and civil war. This revelation was made to the leftist review, *Militancia,* edited in Argentina by the former Sub-secretary General of MAPU, Eduardo Aguevedo.

"Friday the 7th and Saturday the 8th of September," relates Aguevedo, "I took part in a meeting with Allende and the heads of the political parties of the U.P. We discussed the question of a coup. . . ." That a definite plan of action had been agreed upon, that the decision to follow through with it had been taken, may be the case, but no one can claim for certain that a definite Plan Zeta existed, judging solely on the evidence presented in the White Book.

From my personal experiences and from what I know of the situation I cannot vouch for the truth of Plan Zeta as presented in detailed form by the Military Junta. I don't say that the plan did not exist. It may have existed. I only say that the proofs adduced to prove the authenticity of it are not forceful enough to convince one that Plan Zeta without doubt existed and was going to be put into action. It appears, however, that some plan existed. I base this conclusion on the following:

1. *Before September 11:*

(a) A priest member of the steering committee of MAPU told me confidentially that the U.P. had arms for 50,000 persons.

(b) Members of the U.P. assured me of the existence of plans, defensive and offensive, in the sectors where they were living.

(c) Again I was told that members of the U.P. in two critical situations had mounted guard in their *población* and had received orders to meet at specified points to pick up arms at a prearranged signal.

2. *After September 11:*

(a) The declarations made to me by a young man, relative to the paramilitary preparations he had received as a member of a government defense organization. He had come to solicit my help to enter an embassy as a political refugee.

(b) Confirmation of these declarations by another older man, relative to the plans of defense of the government. He also asked for help to enter an embassy.

(c) Fabrication of arms in some of the industries taken over by the state. For example, in Madeco small tanks were secretly being built; in Mademsa, anti-tank rockets; in Fensa, plastic anti-tank mines; in Carrocerias Franklin, rockets.

(d) A story, by a priest known for his good judgment and prudence, to the major superiors of religious congregations at a one-day seminar in Santiago. He said that on the 11th, very shortly after the coup began, an ex-priest and his wife had sought refuge in the rectory of the parish where the ex-priest used to be a curate. His wife broke down in hysterics. After calming down a little, she told the priests that the Armed Forces would kill her. "They will surely find in my house," she said, "the list of people I was supposed to kill according to the orders received from the U.P."

(e) A personal experience. One day I received a telephone call from a woman whom I had not seen since she had been a student in the junior college where I used to be rector in Antofagasta. She said that she urgently needed to see me. I told her to come at once to the rectory. "I can't," she replied. "Please meet me in the back of a garage at 474 X Street."

I understood immediately that she was in trouble with the military government and I told her I'd be there in no time. The Junta forces were not looking for her but for her husband. She asked me to find asylum for him in an embassy. That same night I called at the home of an ambassador I knew. I told him the story as I understood it. He needed more details. I left and in the wife's company went to where her husband was hiding. I asked him point-blank his name, occupation and party affiliation. He gave me his full name and said that he was an *interventor* in a canning factory. As for his party affiliation he said that he belonged to the Socialist Party — to its extremist group headed by Altamirano.

Then I asked him directly, "Why is the military government after you?"

"They accuse me of illegally making bombs instead of canning food," he replied.

I asked, "Is it true?"

"Yes, Father, it's true," he replied sheepishly.

"What will they do to you if they catch up with you?"

"They'll line me up before a firing squad."

The next day I returned to the embassy. The man received asylum and today both he and his wife are in a new country.

(f) Another personal experience: One day in October 1973, I accompanied a priest to 1161 Santa Rosa Street, a building directly in front of the Arriarán Hospital. The building, owned by the Congregation to which my companion belonged, was called *Casa de Comunidad Juveniles* (Community Youth Center) and had been leased to the *Servicio Nacional de Salud* and the University of Chile. The person in charge was Dr. Luis Wernstein, a psychiatrist from Arriarán. Dr. Luis and his collaborators had taken complete possession of the building. They stopped paying rent and had begun proceedings to have the state expropriate it. On that visit, I learned that the building had been used by foreign extremists not only as a community center but also as a workshop for the planning of a civil war and the taking of absolute power by the U.P., judging from the documents found hidden there.

All these strands point to the definite fact that a plot was being weaved. They do not point conclusively to the existence of the so-called Plan Zeta. But taken together they point to something at least resembling an overall plan. Even more they lend credence up to a point to Plan Zeta. Nothing proves conclusively, however, that Plan Zeta as presented did exist or did not exist.

7

Plan Zeta in Reverse

The Military Junta is the target of criticism, especially as regards tortures, from all the corners of the
world, from men of renown in the fields of education,
politics and religion, and organizations of all kinds.

This chapter will examine this problem in the
most objective way possible. It will present a series of
pertinent general data, then a national picture of the
unemployment problem resulting directly from the
military coup — then continue with the subject of
tortures in general and in particular with a listing of
twenty cases, and finally the conclusion.

GENERAL INFORMATION

1. *For the Whole of Chile:*
(a) Number of persons killed due to the events

on and subsequent to September 11: between 3,800 and 5,000.

(b) Number of people who disappeared: 300.

(c) Number of people arrested — 30,000. This number does not include those detained in camps of concentration, as for example Dawson, Pisagua, Chacahuco, Quiriquina, Putre. As of September 15, 1974, 8,000 persons were still detained for political reasons.

(d) Tortures — between thirty and fifty percent of those arrested are tortured once or twice or more, and many of them remain incommunicado, sometimes for as long as two or three months.

(e) Trial — notification to defense lawyer only one or two days before the trial. In practice, it is very difficult if not impossible for the accused to avail himself of a lawyer.

(f) People dismissed from work between November 12 and December 24, 1973: 28,310.

(g) People out of work: from 270,000 to 350,000 in a work force of three million, as of September 15, 1974.

(h) Population of Chile: around ten million.

2. *In Santiago:*

(a) Number of people killed due to the events on and subsequent to September 11: between 1,500 and 2,000.

(b) Number of persons in jail in Santiago for political or security reasons: 6,000; 2,900 of these are awaiting trial; from eighty-five to ninety percent of them were imprisoned without trial. Centers in Santiago where they are held prisoner: Bastilla, San Bernardo, El Bosque, etc.

UNEMPLOYMENT

Data supplied by the Department of Labor on dismissals from work as registered in its offices throughout the country: These numbers correspond to persons dismissed from work in the private sector between November 12 and December 24, 1973. They do not include those laid off in the public sector nor the cases registered in the special tribunals of the Department of Labor.

Tarapaca	2,214
Antofagasta	1,453
Atacama	251
Coquimbo	1,248
Aconcagua	1,002
Valparaíso	2,749
Santiago	9,923
O'Higgins	251
Colchagua	193
Curico	106
Talca	436
Linares	145
Maule	303
Nuble	796
Concepción	2,139
Arauco	111
Bio-bio	910
Malleco	589
Cautin	410
Valdivia	1,160
Osorno	420
Llanquihue	107
Chiloe	50

Aysen 155
Magallanes 1,189
TOTAL 28,310

Thousands have been dismissed from their work for the sole reason of: (a) belonging to the Communist, Socialist or to the MAPU Political Party; or (b) having been given work in the public sector during Allende's term of office.

EFFECTS OF UNEMPLOYMENT
IN THE PRIVATE SECTOR

1. *Unemployment:* A person dismissed from his job receives no compensation if the cause of his dismissal falls within Law decree No. 32 or if the dismissal is the consequence of inappropriate conduct.

2. *Health:* If a person loses his job, he and his family are deprived of the gratuitous services associated with the *Servicio Nacional de Salud* (the National Health Services).

3. *Housing:* Sumar, Yarur (textile mills), Madeco and a few other industries require that the house of the company in which lived the worker dismissed from the company be evacuated in the briefest time. In the case of the three companies just mentioned, one must bear in mind that these houses were built with the proceeds of a five percent tax levied on the companies for housing and the payments made by the workers themselves.

4. *Retention of Salaries:* In the majority of the companies, when the worker is arrested, the family

receives no allowances, even if the worker is not laid off.

5. *Indemnization:* No company yet has completely paid to a person, laid off from work, the salary of one month for every year of service rendered as demanded by the law.

EFFECTS OF UNEMPLOYMENT IN THE PUBLIC SECTOR

1. *Retirement:* The employees of the National Health Service who are dismissed from their jobs lose their seniority in the service and in consequence are deprived of adequate pension funds.

2. *Maternity:* The laws in this matter have not been respected.

3. *Unemployment Compensation Funds:* None in the public sector wholly dependent on the state.

4. *Access to Pertinent Information Denied:* The Ministry of Agriculture, of Housing, of Public Works, the State Technical University, Endesa (the State Public Utilities Company), *Banco del Estado* (State Bank), Civil Registry prohibit the workers dismissed from their job access to the place where they used to be employed and refuse to give them pertinent information as to the exact reasons for their dismissals.

5. *Withholding of Salary:* In the State Bank and in the offices of the General Treasury of the Republic *(Tesoreria General de Republica),* employees are laid off without any right to any salary whatever or to any compensating fund.

6. *Arrests and Dismissals:* The persons arrested

and dismissed from the M.O.P.T. (Ministry of Public Work and Transport), the Civil Registry and the State Bank receive no allowances for their families (actually this is becoming more and more general and is true of almost all of the public sector).

7. *U.T.E. (State Technical University) and M.O.P.T.:* These refuse to give to the workers the documents required by the agencies that give financial help. All the actual construction projects of the Ministry of Housing have been transferred to the private sector with the stipulation of contracting the same personnel under contract with the public sector. The new construction companies on taking over the construction jobs from the public sector immediately give to a sizable number of these construction workers a thirty-day notice to the effect that their contract will be cancelled.

NUMBER OF PEOPLE LAID OFF IN THE PUBLIC SECTOR

S.N.S. (National Health Service) — 15,000.

DINAC — 2,400 to 2,500.

ODEPLAN (mostly technicians and professionals) — 164.

ENAP — 500.

INDAP — 1,200.

U.T.E. (State Technical University: professors and administrative personnel) — 1,200.

The major legal reasons adduced for the termination of the working contracts in both the private and the public sectors are (in decreasing order of importance) the following:

(a) Law decree No. 32, art. 4, October 4, 1973.

(b) General Law 16.455.

(c) Oral notification of termination of work contract; no specific reasons given.

(d) Pressures by the companies on workers to give up their jobs and their benefits.

Law decree No. 32 refers to the emergency situation in the country and the necessity of reestablishing the principle and the practice of labor discipline. It refers to those who supposedly had been the instigators of illegal strikes and acts of violence.

Law No. 16.455 is the basic general law in which is stipulated the legal grounds for dismissal of workers, for example, failure to show up for work, misbehavior, incompetence, etc.

The following companies, among others, invoked Law decree No. 32: American Screw, Alfa Autos, Madeco, Plansa, National Tobacco Company, Acrolite, Plastinud.

Those invoking General Law 16.455 included: Graham Wholesale Company, Gasco, Inacap, Endesa, Quimantu, Enap.

Among those giving oral notifications were: Hotel Sheraton, Sumar Textiles, Caupolican Textiles and Scappini Men's Shop.

The following companies pressured their employees to resign: Copihue Canning Factory, Savory Ice Cream, CIC, Rayon Said.

TORTURES

Granting that the international press was not careful and scrutinizing enough, that it was still under the spell of the image created by Allende and consequently unconsciously biased in its reporting of the situation, are not the charges of summary executions and torture, although much less than actually reported, nevertheless true in many instances? Yes. There have been arbitrary arrests and looting, torture and summary executions.

I know definitely of seven from Antofagasta (not reported by the press) who were tortured and subsequently killed. The motives and causes I do not know definitely as yet. But that they were tortured and killed I know and hold as an indisputable fact. I also know for certain that in Pisagua, in Santiago (*Estadio Chile,* for example), in Calama, La Serena, Coquimbo and Talca hundreds of people were tortured and killed. In Calama, twenty-six were executed on orders of General Sergio Arrellano Stark, the military commander of Santiago at this writing. All of them had stood trial before and had been given sentences ranging from two months to twenty years in jail. Nevertheless, they were executed one by one in the presence of those waiting their turn to be killed.

Citizens of other countries were killed: Frank Teruggi, a student from the United States; Jorge Rios, a Bolivian studying at FLACSO, tortured and then killed; Edmundo Horman, a film producer from the U.S., among others.

PSYCHOLOGICAL TORTURES

There are physical tortures but there are also psychological tortures. In the *Estadio Nacional* of Santiago, at least once that I know of, a group was forced to face a firing squad. They were not hurt physically for the shots were blanks only, but psychologically they were traumatized.

In Pisagua they nailed prisoners in barrels and told them that they were going to bring them to a high hill near the sea and then roll them down into the sea. They rolled down but never reached the ocean, yet these people were psychologically marked for the rest of their lives.

Also in Pisagua, they forced a man to hit his own brother who was also a prisoner there. To another, after torturing him they asked him if he preferred to be shot facing or with his back to the firing squad, and to whom should his corpse be sent — to his mother or his wife. Afterwards, blindfolded they left him to walk around in circles for four hours. Every now and then, soldiers would punch him in the face, in the abdomen and in the back. At irregular intervals, he would feel the barrel of a revolver on the nape of his neck and hear the click of the gun.

FALSE MILITARY COMMUNIQUES

Also reprehensible is the manner in which the Armed Forces attempt to conceal tortures and killings. On numerous occasions the public is notified by official communiques that prisoners are killed trying to escape. The scenario is, however, so identical in all the cases that more and more people are beginning to doubt its authenticity. In every case, the vehicle in which the prisoners are being transported suffers a breakdown and the prisoners, taking advantage of the situation, try to flee. The result is that the soldiers have to kill them.

Probably, this has happened a number of times, but it is difficult to believe that regularly the same incident, even in its minutest detail, repeats itself in such a fashion. The truth of the matter in many of these cases is that the military prisoners are told that if they do not escape from the vehicle they will be killed. Evidently, the only alternative is to get away as fast as possible. Unhappily, they are gunned down anyway. The newspapers print the news as released by the official military communiques: "Killed while trying to escape."

On December 22, 1973, the Armed Forces changed the scenario. They concocted an incredible show to explain the death of five terrorists whom they claim were killed in a running gun battle with an Army patrol while trying to blow up a series of high-tension towers between Valparaíso and Santiago. Here is the official communique of the Armed Forces:

"Last night, Friday, December 21, at about 11:30, a military patrol on a routine mission in the northern sector of Santiago, came unexpectedly upon a group of persons at the foot of a high-tension electric tower. Instead of identifying themselves as they were ordered by the military patrol, they opened fire. A fierce battle ensued. Five extremists were killed and two soldiers were wounded. The names of the extremists are the following: Alejandro Patricio Gomez Vega, 22 years old, single, vendor in open-air markets, residence *población* La Ligua...." [It goes on to list the rest.]

There is no truth in this official communique except for the names and addresses of the persons killed. The persons were in jail or already killed by the military when the sabotage was supposed to have taken place. One had been arrested three days before and two others two days previous. For example, Alejandro Patricio Gomez Vega was taken into custody on December 18, and died on December 20, the day before the supposed sabotage took place. The Armed Forces in writing up such deceitful, dishonest official communiques is quickly losing all credibility.

VICTIMS OF TORTURE

Case No. 1: Jorge Pinto, 24 years old, electrician, student in electronics, was arrested with his brother, Jaime, the morning of October 11, 1973, at his home. He was savagely pushed into a jeep in which there were already four soldiers. They drove him to a lonely spot on a hill in Lonquen and ordered him to dive in the water below. They shot him dead as he appeared on the surface. His corpse was found in Parcella 79.

No. 2: Saturday, January 17, 1974, in the afternoon, two friends, Juan Cruz and Pablo Vicente, 28 and 25 years old respectively, both married and living in the *población* Elias de la Cruz, formerly Malachias Concha, one a bus driver on the Cathedral line and the other the owner of a small shop where he assembled and made boxes, together went for a beer in one of the small restaurants of the *población*.

There a notorious delinquent joined them. A soldier, in civilian attire, spotted him and immediately rushed to the local community telephone and asked for a military patrol. By the time they arrived in their jeep, the delinquent had left. The military questioned the two friends. They wanted to know where he could be found. The two friends said that they did not know, that they had casually met him at the beer parlor and really did not know him.

The military did not believe them and tortured them for several hours. In the morning they set them free but on the condition that they would not speak of what happened and that if they had to go to the hospital they would declare that they had had a fight with hoodlums. The two of them suffered broken ribs, crushed fingers, swelled testicles and numerous bruises on their whole body.

No. 3: Jorge Peña Illench, of La Serena, 45 years old, founder of a famous and internationally known philharmonic orchestra exclusively composed of young people and sympathetic to the left-wing cause, was shot to death with others on October 12, 1973. He had already been sentenced to two years of imprisonment by a war tribunal. Apparently, he was executed for having taken his philharmonic orchestra on an engagement to Cuba.

No. 4: The dentist of a workers' union of the state-owned telephone company in Valparaíso, 34 years old, was executed without trial, twenty-four hours after having been arrested.

No. 5: On October 20, 1973, at 2:30 in the morning on the outskirts of Santiago, the police scaled the wall surrounding the property of Gustavo Maldonato and, forcing entry into his house, arrested him. They put him in an ambulance and sped in the direction of a farm known as the "5th of April." On October 21, the 11th Police Commissariat informed his wife that her husband was dead and that she should remove the corpse from the morgue on La Paz Avenue. His body had been found along with two other bodies in the above-mentioned farm of "5th of April." The left part of his face had been completely blown away.

Two detectives presented themselves at noon on October 30 at the home of the widow and expressed their sympathy, adding that her husband had been shot by mistake.

On November 15, the widow, summoned by the police, declared that an "insane lieutenant of the police precinct of Nogales had had a hand in the killing of her husband."

No. 6: Same as in Case No. 5 except that the corpse of a bachelor, age 26, was found on the Los Pajaritos farm.

No. 7: Carlos Berger Guralmik, 29 years old, married, one child of eight months, lawyer and journalist, in charge of the economic section of the Communist daily newspaper of Santiago, *El Siglo.* He had been sentenced to sixty days in jail by a military tribunal. On orders of General Sergio Arrellano Stark, he was executed in Calama.

No. 8: Pedro Correa, electrician at Implatex Company, married, two children, with residence in the *población* Brasilia of Santiago. Unemployed since September 19, 1973. On November 19 he was arrested at his home and brought to the Regiment of San Bernardo in Cerro Chena. His corpse was identified by his brother-in-law on November 26 at the Legal Medical Institute. He had been tortured and then shot to death. His nose was broken, his ears and genitals badly bruised, his body covered with cigarette burns.

No. 9: On September 28, an accountant of the El

Peral Sanatorium was arrested at his work by a military patrol. He was carrying at the time on his person all his personal documents.

His corpse was brought to the Legal Medical Institute on October 4 by a military patrol. They explained that they had found the body along a road. No personal documents could be found on him.

According to a group of other prisoners of Chena (a center notorious for its tortures and not far from Santiago) on October 4, soldiers took a group of prisoners outside with them. On their return they whispered to the other prisoners that one of their group had been killed. The only one of the group who did not return was the accountant of the El Peral Sanatorium.

No. 10: Juan Arce, of the *población* John Kennedy of Santiago, a student and a director of the JAP (an organization in Allende's government at the *población* level for the control of prices of consumer products and their distribution) was arrested at 7:30 p.m. at his home along with three other young men of the *población.* A revolver was found in the house by the soldiers. In *Investigaciones* the four of them were tortured. On December 17 their parents were able to visit them briefly in jail. On December 21 they were killed while being transported from jail to the military regiment in Buin.

No. 11: Pedro Carvajal, a young man of 21, was arrested at his home in Santiago on December 20 by a group of civilians in a pick-up truck. The police and *Investigaciones* claimed they knew nothing of the case. On Saturday, December 22, his parents learned of his death in the newspapers. On Sunday, December 23, at the Legal Medical Institute, they identified him. He had his head crushed, a broken arm, his nails plucked. No trace of bullet wounds were visible. Peter was a textile worker in Sumar and a Jocist, that is, a member of the Young Christian Worker Movement. He belonged to no political parties nor to any extremist movement of the right or left. He was apolitical.

No. 12: In Magallanes, the extreme southern part of Chile, Ernesto Mendez, an elementary-school professor was asked to present himself to the military authorities on September 11, 1973, at the military regiment Caupolican in Puerto Porvenir. After three days of detention he was set free.

On October 22, he was asked once more to present himself to the same military authorities at Puerto Porvenir. He was held there six days. Presumably on the seventh day they shot him for having in his possession a 100-peso bill (these bills were presumed to be connected to Plan Zeta and those in possession of them, *Miristas* — revolutionary extremists). The widow was not given permission to see the body.

No. 13: Alberto Sanchez, 28-year-old father of three children, night guard at the copper mine in Chuquicamata, ex-GAP (member of Allende's personal guard), on October 29 was brought from Calama to the Penitentiary of Santiago. He had been condemned to a 25-year prison term for malversation of funds. Members of his family petitioned in Antofagasta that the case be reviewed. Not long after, they learned that he had been shot to death.

No. 14: On September 22, 1973, Ines Pardo Rojas, a student, unmarried, four months pregnant, was arrested and sent to jail in San Antonio. She had presented herself voluntarily to the military authorities when she was told by a friend that they were searching for her. She ended up in a concentration camp. In San Antonio she was tortured: electrical shocks were applied to the vagina. Medical experts said there was a strong possibility that at birth the child would show the effects of the tortures.

No. 15: In Paine, about fifty kilometers from Santiago fifty-two farmers from nine cooperative farms *(asentamientos)* were arrested by military forces from San Bernardo. As of this writing, except for eight of them, the relatives and families of the forty-four other farmers, after having done everything they could possibly do to locate them, are still ignorant of their whereabouts. As for the eight, they were found dead, blindfolded, scattered in the fields of the nearby farming town of Pirque.

No. 16: On December 15, at 8 p.m., two armed civilians burst into the home of Enrique Infante in the *población* 10 de Mayo, Santiago. They drove him blindfolded in a blue pick-up truck to the 6th Commissariat. They whipped him and gave him electric shocks during the interrogation to which they submitted him. They sent him home warning him not to speak about the tortures inflicted on him.

No. 17: On September 25, in Santiago, a young man of 21, Roberto Larrain Vera, under medical care, was arrested in his apartment at 7 p.m. by a group of eight policemen under the command of a police lieutenant, drunk and with a heavy firearm in his hands. His cousin, Anibal Prieto Larrain, who was visiting with him at the time, was also arrested and taken into custody. Both were brought to regimental headquarters where for fourteen days they were kept blindfolded, whipped and given electric shocks.

On October 10, they were brought to the National Stadium. Five days later, they were transferred to the Penitentiary of Santiago where they are incommunicado.

No. 18: Lucia Gomez, 27-year-old teacher in the secondary school system of Concepción, active member of the U.P., arrested in her home and brought to jail. There she was whipped and her body covered, especially her breasts, with electric burns. Released later.

No. 19: Roberto Cortes, 52-year-old resident of Santiago, arrested by detectives in his home. The two arresting officers immediately understood that an error had been made. The man they were looking for was supposed to be only 25 years old. Nevertheless, they had to follow the orders of the summons. He was kept three days in a cell too small for him to stand up or lie down in and filled with human excrement. No food or liquid was given to him during this time. Liberated on the morning of the fourth day.

No. 20: Mrs. Alejandro Vicuna, a widow, 61 years old, of the *población* La Legua, Santiago, was arrested three times and brought to military headquarters for questioning about twelve hours each time. They wanted to find out where her youngest son, 29 years old, single, member of the paramilitary group of the U.P., trained in Cuba, was hiding.

CONCLUSION

There is no doubt that people are being tortured

and killed in Chile by the military. Tortures have no justification in our civilization. They should never take place. Tortures and summary executions are not ethical, much less Christian.

It is true that there are extenuating circumstances. The country is under military rule as in time of war. The military forces are still smarting from the innumerable ways used by the Allende regime to literally get rid of them. The propaganda by MIR against them, the mutiny of men in the Navy due to three top men of the U.P., and so on. Plan Zeta supposedly contemplated the killing of military officers and their children. These circumstances may explain in part, but they do not justify the conduct of the Armed Forces.

The tortures, physical and psychological, are indeed an aberrance on the part of the Armed Forces and are difficult to understand. The Armed Forces don't realize that they are putting into execution what they claim the U.P. was going to do and therefore putting themselves on the same level — a level of immorality, of degradation from which, they claim, the Chileans were delivered by the Armed Forces.

8

The Military Junta's
Politico-Economic Policies

The Military Junta is aware of the urgent need of profound changes in economics and politics if Chile is not to run the risk of going once more through an ordeal similar to the Allende agony.

As regards economics, the Junta knows very well, for example, that capitalism in Chile is different from the capitalism of advanced industrial countries. The latter have a system of production in which basically all men share. In Latin America, however, the capitalist system is discriminating; it produces only for a few, not for all. It is a system which exploits the majority in favor of a small minority and gives to a very select group monopolistic control, both economic and political, over the rest of the nation. In Latin America, capitalism is an exclusive system; in industrialized advanced countries capitalism is an all-inclusive system.

In advanced capitalist countries, the political and economic power is diffused among the whole nation; there are, it is true, very strong monopolies which wield tremendous influence but they have to contend with powers, groups, unions (countervailing powers, according to Galbraith) as strong, if not stronger, that keeps them in line with the interests of the nation as a whole. John P. Powelson points this out in his book, *Latin America* (McGraw Hill).

In Latin America in general the economic and political power is in the hands of a small minority; the masses don't have any economic or political power, and are subject in consequence to the whims and abuses of the powerful few. The majority live in a condition of dependence on the good will of the reigning elite.

The laws of the market economy in countries of Latin America are not subject in practice to superior laws of solidarity, human fraternity and development of human beings as persons. The prices of commodities are very often set in such a way as to foster exploitation. In general in Latin America, the mechanics of profit render the capitalist system amoral if not immoral. For these reasons the Military Junta is eager to change the existing capitalist system in Chile, to correct its abuses and introduce a capitalism similar to that of advanced industrial societies.

The starting point of the Military Junta in Chile as regards the political life of the country is the whole nation, not a group but the totality of all the persons constituting the Chilean nation. It has taken a definite stand against oligarchic political parties and Marxist-inspired parties which divide, dominate and oppress the masses.

The role of the military in government is rejected by liberal ideologues who look upon the military as the cancer of Latin American politics; by those of the right who resort to the military in the hour of peril but once they are no longer in danger, insist that the soldiers go back to their barracks and keep busy exclusively with military affairs; and by Marxists and those of the extreme left who claim that only the proletariat can play the role of agent in profound structural changes.

The Military Junta has initiated a frontal attack against the political parties in Chile which placed the good of the party and of its members before the common good of the country and of the masses. Its aim is to do away at least for a time with political parties which turned democracy into a sham system. Formal democracy as a political system and a framework for economic development has been a resounding failure in Latin America. The pluri-party system of democratic governments has not been able to promote the common good in Chile.

The political parties of the right were incapable of discerning the aspirations of modern man; those of the center put in practice the interests of their own parties ahead of those of the nation; the Marxist-inspired political parties, although dedicated in word to economic development and political participation, nevertheless *de facto* were too dogmatic and utopian to be agents of development and true political participation.

Even today, with all that happened in Chile, party politics of the lowest kind are not at all over. It is very understandable then that the Military Junta plans to put an end at least for some time to the existence and activities of political parties and substitute a kind of tutelar democracy to replace the democracy existing in Chile.

The model of tutelar democracy which the Military Junta is actually concentrating on is a model of supervised democracy based on the economic and social participation of everyone at all the levels of decisions and actions.

The Junta expects that this variant of democracy, as participation extends itself in all spheres and at all levels, little by little will develop into a model of nonsupervised democracy, of true and strong democracy which can solve the conflicts at a level above the party level, at the level of Chile as a nation.

The objective of the Armed Forces is once and for all to eliminate the existing dualism between the elite on the one hand and the masses, characteristic of the oligarchic political parties, and on the other to reject likewise the Marxist political parties for which the masses are mere objects to be manipulated at will by the elite of the party. Thus, it is that the Junta affirms that all the members of society not only have the right to, but must assume the obligation of taking an active part in a responsible manner in the making of decisions and in the distribution of material goods and social services in order to achieve the fulfillment of every member of the community.

The Armed Forces have determined to modify the fundamental structure of power; they intend to change it not just partially but rather restructure it globally, to operate an authentic transformation of the global process of decision-making in order to effect far-reaching changes on behalf of all the Chileans. Their aim is to effectively help the masses to liberate themselves from the paternalism of the governments of the right and the political parties of the left and develop themselves as free, active and responsible agents in the making of their own history.

To be able to play the role of agents of socioeconomic and political changes, of true and total liberation, the Armed Forces realize that they will have to commit themselves with the nation as a whole not only in words but in deeds and in a special way with the poorest.

If they do not identify themselves with the nation as a whole they will never become agents of social change. In practice, it means that they must be anti-establishment, anti-Marxist and pro-masses, opposed to the conservatives of the right and to the Marxists. Both claim to be in favor of the masses but they are definitely not; they are bureaucrats interested above all in power for themselves; at bottom they are interested in the masses as a means to assure themselves of political power.

The Military Junta recognizes the necessity of a plan of action at the level of participation and at the level of symbolism to legitimize itself and to accomplish these changes.

LEVEL OF PARTICIPATION

At the level of participation, the Junta realizes that many of the difficulties it will have to face stem from the institutional nature of the Armed Forces themselves. The system of authority, of command, of action in all the Armed Forces in the world pivots around a vertical hierarchical axis; the horizontal level of interrelationships is neglected. Authority comes from on high vertically passing from one echelon to the one below according to a prescribed course. Although authority is diffused throughout the institution, it functions monolithically, vertically from the commander-in-chief to the generals, and from them to the colonels and from the colonels to the majors, and so on down the line.

It is no small task to change a way of life conceived in terms of vertical authority to one planned in terms of participation. To be successful in their plans to bring about massive participation, the Armed Forces will find it necessary not only to get rid of a set of mental habits regarding the notion and practice of authority but will necessarily on the level of execution have to create institutions that assure an active, functional participation of all the Chileans not only as regards national objectives but also as regards local aims at the level of work, profession and neighborhood.

The Military Junta acknowledges that true democracy cannot be achieved without the active and real participation of the masses. Its aim, therefore, is to create institutions which make participation real, effective, concrete, in which the masses perceive that they themselves and their children and the whole nation are doing something unquestionably worthwhile.

The political system in Chile from the very beginning of independence up to now, including the government of Allende, has underestimated in practice the value of participation. With the exception in part of some governments, as for example that of Frei, a minority has always concentrated the economic, political and cultural power in its own hands strictly in terms of its own interests. The masses were effectively barred not on the institutional level but on the practical level from active participation in social, economic and political decisions. Even in the decisions that affected them in a very personal way, they (themselves and their family, their work and their daily activities) they were without voice. The masses were never incorporated into society; they never had access to the decision-making mechanisms as regards the life of the nation as a whole, or their own life.

At times, it is true the oligarchs, in certain special circumstances, did share with them the task of planning the future. But true, real participation in theory and in practice never existed under them. And neither did it exist under Allende, even though his slogan was that the masses were the government. They really did not participate more than before.

As Hugo Toro, a union leader, says: "During the government of Allende, the workers were constantly deceived. The participation that the government assured the whole world with great publicity was ours, was not an effective one. We took part in the Councils of Administration, sure, but only as decorative figures. We never had any true power of decision; we were called upon to approve what already had been decided by Corfo or the directors of the Textile Committee. We did not participate; we were used."

The duality of the society in Chile, that is, the coexistence of a small sector in which is concentrated the economic and political power alongside a large sector of marginals with no power, makes participation of all very difficult if not impossible. Decisions which fundamentally affect society are taken by minority groups and not by the majority. There is no effective participation of all and by all neither in the social nor in the politico-economic field. The minority who control the political and economic power and the means of production have set up political and economic institutions to promote and defend their own interests and not those of the nation as a whole. The political model drawn up by the oligarchs or the Marxists under Allende opposed, if not in theory at least in practice, participation by the majority on an effective level.

The objective of the Military Junta is to eradicate the actual lack of participation of the majority and to substantially alter the political structure of power and of political parties. Its aim is to establish institutional mechanisms whereby the majority will be afforded the opportunity to participate directly in political power and not be restrained to token participation as before. On the economic level it aims to arrive at a real pluralism and a more just income distribution. It has set in motion a series of measures in agriculture, mining and industry destined to increase the role of the ordinary worker in decisions affecting him politically, economically and socially.

It intends to decentralize and to give to the local community much more real power, plus responsibility in planning and financing of local programs and of local activities. The Junta's policy is to give to the small communities the opportunity to enter the mainstream of the economic and political life of the nation, to permit them direct access to the programs that affect them personally and to grant effective participation in and control of the decisions which affect them at a local and national level. The Junta is determined at the level of policy to give to every Chilean the means to effectively participate at all levels.

SYMBOLIC LEVEL

The Junta is conscious of the fact that to achieve success it is necessary not only to create institutions which promote participation but to propose a series of symbols which mobilize people along those lines. In order to fulfill the objectives of participation, the masses have to be able to connect them to symbols. These have to be presented to them beforehand in such a way that they can interiorize them profoundly. That is why the Junta hopes to be able to associate in the minds of the people symbols related to specific and concrete objectives so that participation becomes not just something exterior to them but truly interior.

It is not a question of manipulation on the part of the Junta but of psychological help to motivate the masses to interiorize the objectives of participation. The symbols, as the Armed Forces are aware, must appeal to transcendental norms and moral principles of unquestionable value as for example, patriotism, justice, truth, civic spirit, hard work. The symbols must help the nation to identify the legitimate government with the Junta and the Junta with the legitimate government and the nation with the government. In order for this to become a reality the military leaders must become standard-bearers of these values, if the symbols are to signify what they are supposed to in the first place; if not, the symbols will have an effect contrary to the one intended.

If, for example, the nation as a whole in perceiving these symbols comes to the conclusion that the

Armed Forces are the savior of the bourgeoisie and not of all the Chileans then the symbols will have an opposite effect. Symbols are necessary in order to "conscientize" a nation, but if the symbols are contradicted by the acts of the military then the legitimacy to rule, as claimed for by the Armed Forces, will not be accepted. These symbols, as the Military Junta knows well, will bear fruit on condition that the entire nation clearly sees that there is no discrepancy between the symbols and the actions of the Junta.

This is crucial for the Armed Forces; as time goes on they must legitimize their intervention by their actions in behalf of all the Chileans.

For the moment, one of the most important symbols that the Armed Forces will of necessity have to present to all the people of Chile prior to the symbol of reconstruction is the symbol of reconciliation.

The Military Junta realizes that the symbol of reconciliation, based on concrete specific acts of pardon, is for the time being of extraordinary importance. To eliminate the division among Chileans, the Junta on the symbolical and practical level must show that all the Chileans without exception are guilty in one way or another of what came to pass. The symbol of reconciliation can bring to Chile a new springtime of love, fraternity and justice.

Unfortunately the actions of the Armed Forces betray their intentions. In no way is the military implementing in a practical way its declared programs. As time goes on its deeds are more and more aborting on the practical level what is conceived on an abstract level. The discrepancy between words and deeds is as great as if not greater than that of the Allende regime.

9

Conclusion

As this study draws to a close, one might ask why a compromise of some sort was not found whereby Allende could have managed to survive. In this respect perhaps the Church, the Armed Forces, the Christian Democrats should have done more than they did. However, even if these forces had been completely behind Allende, no one could have saved Allende from his fate except Allende himself.

There is inherent to Marxism, Communism and Marxist Socialism a virus of totalitarianism. Marxists do not allow opposition; e.g., they reject the right of anyone to disagree with the party. They alone possess the truth. They look upon truth as a dynamic process but taking place in a predetermined way and according to set rules and principles. As they consider themselves to be the sole dispensers of truth they devise plans to prevent others from contradicting them. The result is that they cannot but be totalitarian. History for them is being realized, but in such a way that its course cannot be changed; there are no alternatives to the interpretation of history outside of Marxism. The only definite explanation of reality which embraces and at the same time replaces all other historical interpretations is Marxism. As far as they are concerned, no creative thought can exist outside of Marxism. They presuppose that historicity and creativity can only be linked to Marxism.

Thus it was that Allende, a convinced Marxist, could not change or amend his political plans. To do so, Allende, the President of Chile, would have had to reject Allende the Marxist. But they were so united that to separate one from the other would have meant the liquidation of one of the two Allendes.

The Armed Forces had no other alternative. Marxism in the long run is not a liberation but an enslavement. It does not offer a human solution to the problems of mankind. Everywhere today in Marxist-dominated countries man cries out for liberation.

There is no doubt that Allende considered his program as one of liberation. But that was only in theory. In practice it was not; on the contrary it consisted as it were in the long run in subjection to the Party, and the Party in turn to the Central Committee and the Central Committee to the dictator. Surely in theory it presented a system of political and economic participation, of historicity, of liberation, but in practice the masses didn't participate more, nor did they enjoy more historicity nor more liberation than before. Everything continued to come from on high and reached them in as paternalistic a mode as before.

The *roto Chileno* (peasant) described in his color-

ful earthy language the government of the U.P. as
"Gobierno de mierda pero mi gobierno."

There cannot be much doubt that the political
and economic projects of the Military Junta, even
though they are in theory more *desarrollista* (develop-
mentalist) than liberating in nature, offer nevertheless
greater liberation than Allende's program — provided, however, that the military not permit its projects
to be bogged down by inertia or class pressures.

Today in Chile, the Armed Forces constitute in
this precise historical moment, the only decisive force
which can put in motion the means necessary to the
attainment of economic development and real effective democratic participation at all levels.

The entry of members of the Armed Forces on
three successive occasions in the cabinet of Allende
gave them a new perspective of the Chilean reality
and a deep conviction of the urgent need of radical
changes.

With their own eyes they saw the ill effects of bu-
reaucracy, of Marxism, of the inefficiency of the so-
called Chilean Socialists, of the excess of crass politics, of the gradual erosion of identity of the Chilean
nation as such. This, coupled with the new trends in
the world towards more social justice, the powerful
movements of liberation in Latin America, the new
processes of "conscientization" begun by Frei, made
the Armed Forces much more aware than before of
underdevelopment, of the need of social justice, liberation, agrarian reforms, and the like.

The earlier option in which the Armed Forces
considered themselves only and exclusively as defenders of the nation against external enemies and of the
established order gave way to a different viewpoint.

The Armed Forces now look upon themselves not only as the guardians of the nation against aggression by external forces but also as bulwarks against the enemies within the country. They do not regard the role of agents of modernization, or of economic, social and political development, as irrelevant to their profession.

Even though they are convinced of the new role that it has to play, the Chilean military is not as enthused over it as its Peruvian counterpart, for example. It is not as well prepared either for the tasks that confront it as were those of Peru. This is understandable. They were not as exposed to the kind of postgraduate courses in their *Academia de Guerra* (War College) as those of Peru.

The courses followed by the Peruvian officers at C.A.E.M. — *Centro de Altos Estudios Militares* (Center of Advanced Military Studies) — and given by professors from the *Universidad San Andrés* of Lima covered all the major problems in the field of economic underdevelopment and development, and embodied the new ideas on social justice, equal economic distribution, agrarian reform and international trade. The postgraduate courses in development and underdevelopment followed by the officers of the Chilean Armed Forces in their *Academia de Guerra* were not as intensive nor as extensive as those followed by the Peruvian military officers.

They are not as cohesive a group either in respect to the ways to solve the problems of underdevelopment. Those in Peru were sensitized to these problems by a group of professors with advanced ideas and strong unanimity as regards the fundamental necessity of development who formed a team more united by its formation and finality than the corresponding group of professors of the Chilean Armed Forces. The professors at the War College in Chile did not form a team nor did they have a common advanced stance on developmental problems. The Chilean Armed Forces were not influenced as strongly as a group.

The Armed Forces of both Chile and Peru are definitely opposed to party politics, at least of the kind that existed prior to their taking control. Both are concerned over the incidence of problems at the national level on the international scene and vice-versa, that is, the incidence of international problems on the national scene.

The Armed Forces of Chile have probably more in common with those of Brazil than with those of Peru. Both Armed Forces fought the implantation of Marxism by Goulart (Brazil) and by Allende (Chile). Neither one was well prepared for the taking on of its new task. Both are anti-Marxist on the political level, and fundamentally *desarrollista,* liberal capitalist, on the economic level. Nevertheless, neither group looks upon itself as a leader with a radically new social perspective but as a reformist group, nationalistic in scope.

Contrary to the Peruvian, the Chilean Armed Forces have not the pretension of developing a new radical, revolutionary sociopolitical system nor are they as critical in the field of the economics of capitalism and particularly international capitalism as the Peruvian military are. On the other hand, they are more taken up by the problems of social justice and much more open to new solutions to the problems of *marginalidad* and economic equality than their counterparts of Brazil. On this score, they are much closer to those of Peru. It is not in their plan, however, to give a mortal blow to the bourgeoisie as it has happened in Peru, but neither do they have the intention in theory of being as linked to the bourgeoisie as is the case in Brazil.

As those in Peru at the beginning, the Armed Forces are divided as regards certain objectives and especially concerning the means to be used to achieve these ends. (When I use the word "divided," in no way do I want to imply, as the rumors would have it, that there is a profound ideological division among them which could flare up at any moment with great possibility of a counter-revolution by the forces which were behind Allende.) On fundamental points, however, they are very united; the great, great majority is anti-Marxist, anti-partisan politics. If the Armed Forces of Peru, even with the advantage of a basic unitary formation and "conscientization" in C.A.E.M., went through an inside struggle for power between October 1968 and February 1969, the fact that the Armed Forces of Chile as regards their economic and social programs and their implementation are not totally and absolutely united should not come as a surprise.

The Armed Forces are divided in their social philosophy regarding social objectives and the kind of means to attain them. Roughly speaking, they can be divided into two groups: one more or less in accord with the fundamental tenets of social capitalism as in Western Germany, and the other substantially in accord with the conservative theses of the *Partido Nacional* (Liberal-Conservative Party). The first group is partial towards socialization, equality of opportunity, a more equal income distribution, participation and profound reforms in the kind of capitalistic system existing in Chile.

The other group is much more conservative in outlook, interested more in the preservation of Chile as it was before Allende than with necessary social and economic changes. It has a closed, paternalistic mentality, and conceives of power along vertical lines in a rigid, disciplinarian framework and divides society between elitist and non-elitist groups. Already some of the younger officers are identifying themselves with the upper class and at the same time are influenced by their prejudices and outlook on social problems. For the moment at least, the Armed Forces of Chile are divided as regards the meaning of development and the kind of means to attain it. Which group will predominate? Although this conservative faction rules Chile now, it is difficult to predict whether or not it will keep the ascendancy.

For the moment, the ministers and high-echelon advisers are, in the main, part of the *Partido Nacional* or at least very sympathetic to its objectives; for example, Enrique Campos Menendez is a civil adviser to the Junta, and Hector Riesle Contreras, a former president of *Fiducia,* an extremely conservative organization, has just been named Ambassador to the Vatican. The Christian Democrats are on the lower rung of the ladder with practically no role to play.

The Armed Forces, as time goes on, must attempt to prove to the people that their mandate over the country is legitimate so that the programs of reconciliation, participation and economic development that they have put in motion to legitimize their government are not stymied by other forces at work.

For the moment, the Armed Forces have to solve the cases of generals who are reckless, imprudent in the use of power, and who presume that the Armed Forces can continue to rule by the use of power, without the need to legitimize themselves by any other means but brute force.

General Forestier, the highest-ranking military commander in Iquique, is a case in point. Dialogue with him is impossible — even the colonels under him can't converse with him. He considers himself the only authority. He is under the impression that he alone can grasp the truth and that in consequence others cannot say anything approximating the truth if what they advance is not totally, absolutely the same as what he puts forward. He proved to be that kind of man in two deplorable events that occurred in Iquique: one was the exile of Esteban Pierek, a priest, an Oblate of Mary Immaculate, and the other, the death of Father Poblete, a Salesian.

Father Pierek was stripped of his passport and under heavy guard was taken to the Peruvian frontier city of Tacna, Peru. He was accused of being in favor of the U.P. and of having engaged in spying activities for the government of Allende. Everybody in Iquique knew that these charges were false and ridiculous, that Father Pierek was not at all sympathetic to the U.P., much less involved in any way with the government. People of all walks of life tried to tell General Forestier this evident truth. Impossible. In the end they went over his head and fought Father Pierek's case in Santiago and won. Father Pierek was free to return to Chile. When General Forestier found out, he said that the Armed Forces would always be at the priest's heels and that he would expel him once more at a moment's notice, on the slightest grounds of suspicion.

Father Poblete, the Salesian, was dead less than two hours after his arrest. He and a seminarian were watching a football game with binoculars from the roof of the school where they taught. They were seen by soldiers and immediately brought to military headquarters for questioning under the accusation of spying. The Salesian priest was tortured; he was hit savagely with the butt of a gun on the head until he was dead. According to the military report made public the priest had died from the wounds received in a fall when he lost his balance jumping with his hands tied behind his back from the truck to the ground at his arrival at the military headquarters! The report added that he had confessed that he was a Marxist and that persons propagating other versions of this incident would be severely punished.

Father René Ferragne, a Canadian missionary, the pastor of the Gruta de Lourdes in Punta Cavancha, Iquique, was required by General Forestier in a letter sent first to the Bishop of Iquique, Msgr. José Valle, to give a detailed explanation of one of his Sunday sermons. Father Ferragne had heard that some people were rejoicing at the death of five who had been killed in Pisagua, a military detention camp, in the days preceding the Sunday in which he gave the sermon the military authorities requested. In his sermon he had only pointed out that such rejoicing was absolutely unchristian and whoever called himself Christian could not harbor such feelings; if he did he certainly was not a Christian.

The special attention paid to the slum-dwellers;

the exhortation of the Undersecretary of Labor, Lamberto Cisternas, to laid-off workers to denounce those pressuring them to sign documents by which they waive their rights to indemnization; the prohibition of general dismissals; the effective granting of land to farmers; the notification to the former owners of mills, companies and business enterprises in general who had left Chile during the term of Allende and whose property had been seized by the government, that they were not to get back these properties; the decree against mass killing by the Minister of the Interior, subsequent to the protests on the part of lawyers, priests and bishops in relation to the killing of the seven in Antofagasta as mentioned above; and the permission granted to form the first company directed and administered by the workers themselves of Fensa who had been dismissed because of their political ties with the left; these measures show a vivid interest in justice, in participation and in the prosecution of the common good on the part of the Military Junta.

But this is not quite enough as we will presently see. The Armed Forces will have to do much more, if they truly want their programs of reconciliation, economic development and participation to be successful and affix the seal, as it were, of legitimacy to their government.

THE MILITARY AND RECONCILIATION

As regards the project of reconciliation, it is apparent that the Military Junta allows itself to be unduly influenced in many cases by members of the ultra-right wing group of the now discredited *Patria y Libertad* and reactionary groups within the *Partido Nacional,* the Liberal-Conservative Party. The Armed Forces at times seem not to take into account that these two groups are as bad, if not more so, than were the fanatics of the *Unidad Popular.*

Here is an example. The rector of the Colegio San José in Antofagasta, a city of 200,000 in northern Chile, was denounced almost every day for a year by groups of *Patria y Libertad* and extremists of the *Partido Nacional* to the military governor of the province for subversive activities. In their determination to oust the rector, they made use of incredibly devious means. For example, they reported to Military Intelligence agents that there was enough dynamite hidden in the basement of the school to blow up the whole city of Antofagasta. The school was searched thoroughly by police in civilian dress. Nothing was found. The accusation was malicious and unfounded. On another day, two students brought two revolvers to the rector, asking him to accept them. The date specified by the government by which all arms had to be turned in to the local military authorities had elapsed. They claimed that they were afraid to keep them in their home and that they did not dare to turn them in at this time.

The rector refused at first but then at their pleadings changed his mind and took them. Five minutes later, he jumped in the school's Volkswagen and brought the two firearms to the rector of the cathedral. Less than fifteen minutes after, the military rushed into the college in search of illegal possession of firearms.

The rector of the school is strictly apolitical but

the groups of *Patria y Libertad* and extremists of the *Partido Nacional* refuse to share his objective, non-partisan, long-range viewpoint on world problems and the training and development in critical thinking which the school under his leadership tries to foster among the students.

Unjust dismissals from work, persecutions by the military against civilians based on charges of informers, usually people out for revenge, continue. Such conduct is not conducive to reconciliation nor does it convince the Chileans that justice and not military power is the cornerstone on which the new government is supposed to be built.

Tortures also continue. Incredible as it sounds, men like the military vicar and the military chaplains who tend to the sacramental needs of their military flock and high members of the Junta who receive Holy Communion find it not illogical at the same time to condone or at best ignore violence, tortures and killings.

Solutions of a repressive character, such as killings, tortures, jail terms and unjust dismissal from work, are of no value in convincing people that Marxism has nothing to offer. The only solution that goes to the roots of the problem is a political and socioeconomic solution which would transform in all its aspects the Chilean reality. Marxism is neither exclusively nor principally a Russian machination with tentacles in all parts of the world, nor the result of the penetration of agents of Communism from the exterior. The credibility of Marxism in Chile lies in the existing intense economic and social injustices. The rise and success of Marxism is due to the existence of a deeply unjust social order. All interpretations which consider Marxism as the principal effect of worldwide conspiracy on the part of Russia or the effect of the work of external liaison people is simplistic.

In Chile, Communism, Marxism, guerrilla warfare and violence did not come about spontaneously. They are the result of unjust social conditions. A case in point is that of a radio announcer who was sent by the Armed Forces to the detention camp in Pisagua along with thirty-nine other persons from Victoria and Alianza for the sole reason that they were Communists. Victoria and Alianza are two small mining towns of the *pampa salitera* (nitrate fields) adjacent to each other in northern Chile about forty miles from Iquique. The reason that motivated this radio announcer to become a Communist was socioeconomic in nature. He was a radio announcer in Iquique. One day, he began seriously to think about starting a union for radio announcers. Not long afterwards, he was dismissed from his job and as he later was to find out, he was blacklisted from jobs at least in radio in all the other broadcasting stations of Iquique. The underlying reason was that he was a union organizer. The result was that he could not find work and in time became a Communist.

In a society in which a worker loses his job and is permanently out of work in his specialty, essentially because he chanced upon the idea of grouping workers to protect themselves from owners, the obvious and only alternative in a country such as Chile to protest against such a state of affairs is to join the Communist Party. Eventually he was contracted by a group of priests in charge of a radio station in Victoria to be the main announcer of their programs. They gave him work because he was professionally competent. At his new post he was always very discreet; he never mixed politics and work. Nevertheless for the simple reason that he was a Communist, he was arrested and sent to a detention camp.

Another example concerns a farmer in Pirque, a small town in the countryside about twenty miles from Santiago, who voted for Allende and indirectly made propaganda in his favor. His son was a Communist. The two, father and son, were detained on charges of being Communists, for the sole reason of having voted to right flagrant social injustices. Such actions on the part of the Armed Forces will in the long run do them and the country much harm.

Imprisonment and tortures will not change the thinking of people who voted for Allende, or who became Communists in the hope that a new administration would do away once and for all with corruption and social injustices. On the contrary, they will be more confirmed than ever in their political opinion. I think of a young man, 24 years of age, whom I met January 25, 1974, only a few days after being released from a concentration camp. With hatred in his voice, he told me he had quit MAPU and become a Communist. He was convinced that only a violent class struggle could save Chile.

Those sent to jail in Pisagua, only because they were Communists in the presidential era of Gabriel Gonzalez Videla, did not change their minds; in fact they came out more convinced than ever of the justice of their position. Many of the leaders during the term of Allende had been sent to Pisagua by President Videla. Communists are going to change in Chile when social conditions are transformed for the better, not before. No other test is credible in their eyes.

The Armed Forces should examine more deeply the causes of Marxism and Communism in Chile and should eradicate them with countermeasures in politics and economics instead of counting upon the use of repressive means. The use of such measures is the surest and best way for the seeds of Communism to mature. Tortures, killings, arbitrary lay-offs from work, excessive credulity in charges by persons motivated by fanaticism and vengeance do not in any way help the spirit of reconciliation which Chile is in need of so badly at this precise moment. On the contrary, the end result of such actions has exactly the opposite effect: revival of bitter division, antagonism, deepening of the wound instead of healing.

The fanatics of the *Partido Nacional* — their number is by no means insignificant — have a blind faith in the Military Junta. As far as they are concerned the Military Junta is always absolutely right in all its decisions. For example, most members of the *Partido Nacional* don't believe that people are tortured and killed; or if they do, they claim that they deserve it. They are as fanatical as the worst fanatics of *Unidad Popular*, who could not imagine that President Allende could be wrong. In the same way that they indirectly did much harm to Allende, so the fanatics of *Partido Nacional* can in the long run exercise an unwholesome influence on the Military Junta.

They are insensitive to the sufferings of the masses; of those in concentration camps for political reasons; of those who mourn the loss of a brother, or husband, or father in the military take-over. They don't realize that the economic measures — e.g., the lowering of salaries in relation to the cost of living and of the high cost of all articles, including the basic foods — are causing incredible hardships on the poor families of marginal groups. The fact that a poor woman whose husband was killed in a skirmish with a military patrol in a mill has to support her eleven children, leaves them cold. The typical answer of these people is: "It's her husband's fault. Why did he have to get killed?"

This attitude, if not general, is certainly too widespread. They divide society into winners and losers, victors and vanquished. They don't seem to notice that they are doing the same thing which they accuse the former government of doing; they too are dividing the Chileans. Those of *Unidad Popular* used to divide the Chileans into Quislings and patriots, good people and bad. Today these people are dividing the Chileans into victors and vanquished.

"They want to reap the full benefit of the military take-over for themselves exclusively; the rest in their opinion are not worth helping or caring for or encouraging. They don't know how to pardon or how to ask pardon. They can't say no to hate, retaliations and denunciations. They have no compassion for those who suffer, justly or unjustly, and they don't try to alleviate these sufferings. They don't ask the vanquished to participate in the work of reconstructing a new Chile; they don't make them feel that they are needed."

The preceding quotation is from the 1973 Christmas Message of the Bishops of Chile. The original is couched in a more indirect style. I took the liberty of giving it a more direct tone. This version is, I believe, faithful to the original.

Here are a few examples of intolerance. At a

Christmas party in the district where I lived in Santiago, organized by the Christmas Committee of the Seventh District of Santiago, there were present, mingling with others, those who were known to be in favor of *Unidad Popular* and among them former members of the precinct organization. Many of the others, the majority, opposed to the U.P., were not at all happy to see them there and pointedly told them so. As far as they were concerned the U.P. people had no business being there although the only crime they had committed was that they were once sympathizers of Allende.

The rich people in the better-off suburbs are incredibly intransigent and fanatical with those who were in favor of Allende. In Las Condes, a fashionable district of Santiago, the attitude of the victors is sickening. One has to live there or at least to go there often to believe it. It is in the slum districts of Santiago that there is less intolerance between neighbors of different ideological convictions and political affiliation. I don't claim that there was not any fanaticism, intolerance or outright injustices in those poor districts during Allende's period or that there were no brutal vendettas there after September 11. I am saying that in general among the poor, there is more fraternity, friendship and real acts of reconciliation than among the rich in the well-to-do residential districts of Santiago. There are too many well-to-do residents whose hearts are absolutely closed to the sufferings of the former members of the U.P.

The reactions of the great majority to the letter of criticism sent to Father Hasbun, director of the T.V. station of the Catholic University, a hero in Chile for his strong and courageous stand against

Marxism and the government of the U.P., by Bishop Ariztia, Auxiliary Bishop of Santiago, clearly show that they are blind to the sufferings of the poor who voted for the U.P. They do not at all understand the message of the bishop who asked for nothing more than for compassion towards the humbled U.P. followers, restraint in the attacks on the politically vanquished silent majority and the end of a divisive mentality.

There are arbitrary judgments not only in the labor field but also in the judicial area where, for example, there still are secret war councils which, according to the law, should be public. For example, one of the last courtmartials held in Talcahuano textually says, "As of the 17th of this month, after an exhaustive study of the case had been made, the Commander-in-Chief of the Second Naval Zone gave his approbation to the sentence pronounced by the Honorable Courtmartial. The execution of the sentence will take place within the legal time limit for such cases. The sentence pronounced and approved includes two condemnations to capital punishment, forty-one to prison terms varying from twenty-two years to sixty days and two found not guilty." These cases were heard, and the verdicts given in the strictest privacy.

The right to legal protection is violated every day in Chile since the advent of the Military Junta without any protest, at least public, on the part of the judicial powers. The State of Siege or State of War does not in any way cancel this fundamental human right as established in Articles 13, 14, 15 and 16 of the Constitution of Chile. The judicial branch which defended the legal rights of the citizens against the illegal acts of Allende's administration today is silent in the face of the abuses against the right to legal protection on the part of the government of the Armed Forces. The members of the judicial power are thus gravely failing in their duty and are thus lending countenance to the accusations proffered against them by the former political regime, namely, that the judiciaries are the legal defenders of the Chilean bourgeoisie and not of all Chileans.

THE MILITARY AND PARTICIPATION

As regards the system of civilian participation theoretically encouraged by the Military Junta, there is a sizable number of military officers who are not in favor of the idea of real, effective participation. Already in certain organizations it is apparent that the objective is not participation on an effective level. The framework of participation is set up but the contents within it have been altered; there is but an artificial link between the framework and the contents. There is danger that the system of participation drift little by little into a paternally controlled system.

THE MILITARY AND POLITICS

As regards the new perspective on politics there are certain basic postulates expressed by the Armed Forces of which the Chileans in great number do not approve. It is evident that it is urgent that the political atmosphere be cleared before beginning the reconstruction period although one wonders if the two things could not be accomplished at the same time. No doubt politics had given way to corruption, graft and the lowest kind of political action possible. Under the guise of politics, common good was sacrificed time and again to private goals.

There is no doubt that politics in Chile needs to be purified. But politics in the true sense of the word should not be destroyed nor replaced. The political dimension of man, in its true sense, is an essential dimension of man. Political apathy is just as bad as an excess of politics. Doing away with politics leads necessarily to paternalism of some sort, and paternalism under whatever form is bad. The politics of the U.P. fell into paternalism. This is not a reason, however, to conclude that politics always leads to paternalism.

Guilds are presented by the Junta as a solution, but they are not. Moreover, guilds are intimately linked to corporatism which conceals a fundamental conservatism of the type of Salazar in Portugal or Franco in Spain, even though theorists such as Jaime Guzman present them in an up-to-date phraseology. Guilds cannot point to the future; in the past they have been used and have failed. True political parties are still the safest bet for the assurance of democracy.

One must beware of the ill effects of a campaign against politics. It would be fatal if for a very long time — it is not a question here of a temporary measure — political apathy should become a political criterion of the Armed Forces. I say political criterion, for the simple reason that non-politics is a kind of political activity, albeit negative.

There is a terrible political vacuum as of now which is getting bigger and bigger with time. The

Communist Party is the only political party not really affected by the strict ban on politics imposed by the Military Junta. Because of their closely knit organization and party discipline, the Communists can go into hiding and blossom forth when the time comes with all their cadres and grassroots organizations perfectly ready for action and in excellent working order. In a few years the only political force in Chile left intact will be the Communist Party. The Military Junta does not seem to realize that indirectly they are laying the groundwork for a political take-over of Chile in the not-too-distant future by the only prepared political organization — the Communist Party. The young, disenchanted with the Military Junta, will have only one option present before them to serve as a catalyst for their ideals.

There is danger that the younger officers of the Armed Forces little by little come to like power and the politics of non-politics. In the best of systems — military, civil, clerical or what have you — there exists the temptation of setting up a class of powerful and privileged people separate from the others. It is not the case in any way for the moment among the Chilean military but it is a problem that could crop up in the Armed Forces and which they must constantly watch so as not to fall into it little by little and ultimately realize what is happening when it is already too late.

THE MILITARY AND ECONOMICS

In regard to economics, it seems that the Military Junta is influenced by the members of the high bourgeoisie and the Chilean economists either trained at or influenced by the conservative school of economics of the University of Chicago. The government of Allende, even according to Marxists like Bernstein or Fajón, had put aside economic efficiency as a basic social objective with the consequent disastrous economic results that followed. But this is not a reason for falling into the opposite error and making a fetish out of economic efficiency. Economics is for man and not man for economics.

In the first days of economic development, capital was formed by compressing consumption and by savings. In this way enough capital was able to be put into the economy in the form of investment. All that was not investment was looked upon as consumption. Investment and consumption were regarded as antithetical terms. Disregard for the human person was prevalent. Attention was focused principally on physical capital and capital goods, and not on human investment. Industrialization was arrived at but at the expense of the human person, of the poor, of millions of people who were undernourished, uneducated, illiterate. It was the classical capitalist system; wealth, it was presumed, would trickle down in time to the poor. It did. However, this was not due so much to the system as to the technical advances in production, and to the new strength of the unions.

This same classical capitalistic system is actually in use in Brazil. It is working in economic terms but at a great social cost. It hopes that the poor will amass enough crumbs so that later on they too will be able to have a table of plenty of their own.

From a moral standpoint, it is utterly indefensible to use man for economic growth, as though growth was the end *in se* and not man, as though man was for growth and not vice-versa, i.e., economic growth for man. In Chile, the economists behind the economic program of the Military Junta fail to make the distinction between consumption for economic development which in the end is an investment, and consumption for consumption purposes which is anti-investment.

The theory of accumulation of capital in capitalism is based on a false dichotomy between investment and consumption. Today there is no need, in order to accumulate capital, to stress the supposed opposition between the two terms. As Salvatore Schiavo-Campo and Hans W. Singer stress in their book, *Perspectives of Economic Development* (Houghton, Mifflin & Co., 1970): The models of economic development in general play up the opposition between investment and consumption. Investment is presented as productive; consumption as unproductive. In this perspective only investment must be maximized; consumption must be minimized. This is the prevalent thinking in the economy of most developed countries. It is understandable in view of the fact that in developed countries the minimum standards of food, health, education and housing are taken for granted and *de facto* exist.

Investment is thought of in economic terms, in terms of money, in terms of physical goods. Some economists, such as Galbraith and Perroux and many of the younger ones, look upon investment in another light, but on the whole the notion of investment in the minds of capitalist economists in Latin America and in Chile, in particular, among the group working for the military, is restricted to money and capital goods.

In underdeveloped countries, economists should not look upon investment in that light. The context is not the same — the elementary needs of health, housing and education are wanting. Consumption expenses of food and health care are not consumption but investment, for, without these, investments can't produce. These basic consumptions are not consumption but investment in underdeveloped countries.

Increase in production is thought of in developed countries (and unfortunately also in Latin America, including Chile) in terms of capital, input, machines; the increase in the rate of investment is an important factor in the acceleration of growth in developed countries. This is true also in underdeveloped countries but only on condition that a different meaning be given to investment. It should include necessary developmental consumption and investment. A primary source of economic growth is human investment. Investment includes in the underdeveloped countries a human and a strictly economic viewpoint. That is true even for developed countries, but investment is not thought of in that way. Hence, the confusion between investment and consumption as regards developed and underdeveloped countries.

To allocate in underdeveloped countries, such as in Chile, investment only in terms of investment without due regard for basic necessary consumption is economic regression. The welfare needs in the economic models of underdeveloped countries are to be considered as investment and not as a factor detrimental to investment — on the contrary. The distinction used in developed countries of consumption as detrimental to investment can't be supported with regard to underdeveloped countries, such as Chile.

The distinction between consumption and investment as used in developed countries is carried over to underdeveloped countries, to Latin America, to Chile, without proper adjustment to the situation of underdevelopment. It is still considered by the economists of the present Military Junta, at least on the pragmatic level, more important to make large investments in productive enterprises than to increase the level of consumption.

Perhaps not in theory, although this is not so sure, but at least in practice basic material needs of the poor are looked upon by the military and its economists as consumption and not investment. The demands of the middle class *de facto* in the economic models these economists are familiar with have priority over the basic needs of the poor. They prefer, it seems, judging by the economic plans they are putting forth, a high per capita income for some and a low per capita income for many rather than an average per capita income for all, with poverty eliminated.

The prices of basic consumer products are too high in relation to the salaries of the poor. One can see the necessity up to a point in view of the financial straits into which the country had been plunged by the U.P., of stringent measures imposed by a government bent to achieve a rapid economic development. Nevertheless, in the actual circumstances it is not only possible but imperative to raise wages of the poorest groups.

EPILOGUE

In general, there is an enormous discrepancy between the expressed policies of the Military Junta and the realization of these in all fields — economic, social and political. Up to a point, this is understandable. It is not always easy even with the best of intentions to put into practice new social projects, new forms of behavior. But even granting this, the discrepancies are far greater than what they normally should be. There is cause for alarm. If the military regime cannot narrow more closely the gap between what it preaches and what it does, there is danger that it will fail miserabiy in the job that it has taken upon itself to do.

Reconciliation is not working out as it should. In fact, there is less reconciliation today than there was several months ago. This is essentially due to the fanaticism of the well-to-do who are taking the upper hand with vengeance in their hearts and to the military who continue to kill and torture.

On the economic level, the poor are suffering terribly. In spite of declarations to the contrary by the Minister of Economy, the poor are much worse off than they were under Allende and even during the first month of the government of the Military Junta. The rich are getting richer. In theory the Military Junta is for the masses but *de facto* it is not. Contrary to what the military regime asserts, it is siding in practice with the bourgeoisie.

On the social and political level, the military leaders are far from having mobilized the Chileans around the same projects, far from having constituted a government which represents all the Chileans. The Junta still has time to do it but it seems that it is further away from it than at the beginning. By its actions, the Junta is dividing the Chileans. In refusing to accept criticism, it has no way of knowing what is going on at the base. In its approach to participation, except for a very limited number of cases, the Junta is too exterior and dominating. It behaves in a paternalistic fashion instead of encouraging the people to search for solutions by themselves.

The present tragedy of the world consists in that the people on the right and those on the left are closed to alternatives of liberation outside their preconceived modes of thought and ideology. On this score the Marxists are as reactionary as the conservatives. Both deny the possibility of a solution outside their ideological framework. Both deny liberty. The conservatives on the one hand look at history through a back mirror and consider it unchangeable, definitive; on the other hand, the Marxists look at history through the front mirror and consider it dynamic but at the same time predetermined, definitive.

The alternative to the dogma of the left and of the right is based not on the back- or front-mirror view of history but on the plain mirror which reflects man, made to the image of God. Man must be the object and criterion of liberation.

We can only hope that the present Military Junta in Chile takes a significant step in this direction so that man will not look any more either in the front or back mirror to solve the problems of man on this earth but in the person of his brother, the mirror of himself.